LIVING IN THE NEW LEMURIA

Exercises, Practices and Techniques

*Pg #18 32 Good Rules
to live by
As for me though I need
relationships, more than Rules
But rules are OK*

Lauren O. Thyme

Lauren O. Thyme Publishing

Santa Fe, New Mexico

2021

LIVING IN THE NEW LEMURIA: Exercises, Practices and Techniques

For information contact:
Lauren O. Thyme Publishing
www.laurenothyme.com
www.thelemurianway.com
https://thymelauren.wixsite.com/thymely-one
https://facebook.com/lauren.thyme

Jacket/cover photo: lotus-flower-3650472_1920 by Aquamarine_song
and Mt. Shasta © Pixabay.com

Interior and cover design: Sue Stein

Other books by Lauren O. Thyme
Purchase on Amazon, Kindle, and Smashwords

Thymely Tales, Transformational Fairy Tales for Adults and Children, 2nd edition
Alternatives for Everyone: A Guide to Non-Traditional Health Care, 2nd edition
Forgiveness equals Fortune (co-authored with Liah Holtzman), 2nd edition
The Lemurian Way, Remembering your Essential Nature (with Sareya Orion), 2nd edition
Along the Nile, 2nd edition
From the Depths of Thyme
Strangers in Paradise
Cosmic Grandma Wisdom
Twin Souls: A Karmic Love Story
Traveling on the River of Time, a handbook for exploring past lives
Catherine, Karma and Complex PTSD
Delphi and the Greek Warrior

Disclaimer:

The author and publisher acknowledge that the information in this book, classes and exercises are provided "as is." The book is not intended as medical or psychological advice and should not be relied on as a substitute for professional consultation with a qualified healthcare provider familiar with your individual medical needs.

I created YouTube videos for most of this book's exercises. To find them, go to YouTube and type in Lauren Thyme.

＊＊＊

Many thanks to Steve Collins for his hard work as we painstakingly rehearsed, edited and presented the classes, and the many hours we spent editing the subsequent book. I couldn't have done these without you.

Table of Contents

Class 3 Exploring Lemuria from Within

Class 4 Discernment

Class 5 Thoughts and Emotions

Class 6 Words, Beliefs and Focusing

Class 7 Protection, Face of God, Lucid Dreaming

Class 8 Being Psychic & Telepathic, Listening with Compassion

Class 9 Manifesting, Astrology, Karma/Evolution, Voice Fighting

Class 10 Evolution of Consciousness, Blame, Cutting Cords

Class 11 Congruence

Class 12 The Big Picture

LIVING IN THE NEW LEMURIA:

EXERCISES, PRACTICES, AND TECHNIQUES

FOREWORD

Over 20 years ago Lauren, at the behest of her Elders, wrote *The Lemurian Way: Remembering Your Essential Nature* with Sareya Orion. That book continues to attract a loyal following of spiritually focused people who seek the nourishment of a soul dislocated in this ever-increasing materialistic world. The message (as are the exercises in this book) is simple yet profoundly life changing.

It has been my great pleasure to be a first-hand observer and participant in bringing this book forward. It began as downloads to Lauren from her Elders of the content of a series of classes presented via Zoom. The classes began and then developed into what became 12 classes. As this was happening, Lauren continued to receive messages from her Elders. She kept a notebook nearby day and night to write notes on the messages she continued to receive. These notes (downloads from her Elders) were organized into the classes, which then became the chapters of the book you now hold in your hands. As time went on Lauren's Elders continued to insistently prod her to broaden her work, making it clear to her that this information must be shared as quickly as possible.

The urgency to do the work continues. As the Covid pandemic now moves into its second year there is no sign on the horizon that life will return to any comfortable semblance of the old familiar. The pandemic has shone a spotlight on all of the critical issues facing our planet with its nearly 8 billion inhabitants. All of the crises are converging as we deal with the refugee crises because of the wars that continue unabated. The climate crisis continues and becomes worse, which impacts all of us.

One major truth has been evident to me for most of my life: we are all connected. In fact, as Lauren says in the book, "Everything is connected to everything." What happens to any one of us happens to all of us. There is no "away" to escape this mess. If we're going to solve these collective crises the only way is to evolve our way out of it.

This book shines a light on the way to evolve our consciousness: our consciousness as a species, the consciousness of our troubled planet and the consciousness of all the creatures on our planet. We aren't going to do it by going off into our quiet corner in our gated community of the mind. We're all in this together. We need to evolve and quickly. As each day passes the crises facing our planet compound each other. We don't have time to waste.

What does it mean to become a New Lemurian? For starters, it means for each of us to take ownership of our part in this. Beyond that it means to be part of the solution. The exercises presented here offer a way forward: a way to deepen our awareness so that we can be better prepared to do what we are called to do.

Living in the New Lemuria is a crash course in a condensed curriculum for deepening our discernment and awareness; developing unconditional love for self and others; paying attention; becoming better at practicing compassion and empathy; and becoming a joyful co-creator while deepening trust and surrender to a Higher Power. These exercises are powerful while seeming to be simplistic. Think of them as building blocks, tinker toys for the soul. With consistent practice the work of transformation yields dividends.

To quote Lauren, "Many people are experiencing a DNA upgrade because of a worldwide shift in spirituality and ascension. The upgrading of our DNA means that we are unlocking our ethereal DNA, giving us a fully activated

12-strand DNA, which is what the ancient Lemurians had." Gold light is transforming us into becoming New Lemurians.

We are living in a time of rapid transformation on a planet that is overtaxed in the name of profits and conflict as the dualistic nature of 6th Wave (as elucidated by Carl Calleman in his book ,*The Nine Waves of Creation*) calls the tune. Fortunately, we have been in the 9th wave since 2011, assisting us in this process. To fully implement and activate the energy of the 9th Wave is to be born into a new consciousness: the consciousness of the New Lemurian. That is what this book offers. The book is, in essence, an owner's manual as we evolve into a new awareness and a new quantum reality, joyously co-creating. Lauren is an Elder and, in these classes, teaches us to be Elders-in-Training. We have the hardware and software to become Elders and usher in a glorious new world.

Any of these exercises can be done alone; however, they are much more powerful when done as the Lemurians did, sharing group consciousness. That is the true essence of co-creation, a spiritual hallmark of the quantum leap which humanity is in the midst of right now. The ancient Lemurians knew that when powerful spiritual practices were done in a group, the energy grew exponentially.

This simple book offers you a gateway to new worlds and wonderful possibilities. Enjoy the journey!

– Steve Collins

Biography: Steve Collins is learning to be empathic after a lifetime of not fully respecting that aspect of himself. His work experiences have ranged from being caseworker for youth in court-mandated placement in a residential treatment facility to being a motor coach operator, personal chef, and tour guide. Spiritually he has long had a sense that we are all connected and that it's an illusion that we are separate. He came in wired for astrology, which he has used in his life as a language to discuss aspects of consciousness and develop a broader understanding of the human condition.

INTRODUCTION

Living in the New Lemuria is designed to assist you in applying spiritually transforming concepts from *The Lemurian Way: Remembering Your Essential Nature* into your life. You will have an opportunity to download information and practice techniques that the Lemurian Elders (also known as Ascended Masters) want to share with you. At the end of every class chapter, you will join in a group meditation located energetically at Mt. Shasta, a holy mountain in northern California that is one of the remaining sacred sites of Lemuria.

Living in the New Lemuria is based on interactive classes I taught on Zoom with people from all over the world joining in. This book is offered to those who didn't hear about the classes as well as others who are awakening and hungering for more.

Since finishing the classes and as this book was being readied for publication, I came to some clear realizations as to why the Elders urged me to create classes, then this book, and finally asking me to create YouTube videos of the book's spiritual exercises. They continue to stress that "time is of the essence," with not a moment to waste.

Since 2011, as we entered the 9th and final wave of creation according to the Mayan Calendar, I believe we are in process of developing into a new species of human being. This birth process can be intense, painful, arduous, and bewildering. However, this birthing is connected with the Divine and a Divine plan for humans, sometimes called ascension or moving into 5th dimensional

(5-D) experience. The exercises, along with Gold Light as used extensively throughout this book and on my YouTube videos, are highly instrumental in shifting one's consciousness and one's physical body into this new state of being. Spiritual practices such as meditation, yoga, qigong, and aligning with spiritually minded others in unity and harmony also accelerate the birthing of this new human.

Working in and *as* the quantum field helps us to align with the Divine. Quantum physicists are now realizing that our thoughts and attitudes shift our reality into something greater than our former selves and infinitely more positive, something that mystics have known about for millennia.

Our spiritual teachers are talking about the same issues as I have written about in this book. Here are a few quotes from some of them:

> "...when we are fully in resonance with the Ninth Wave, our lives will not be about running separate individual agendas, but about fulfilling an aspect of the divine plan for humanity."
> – Dr. Carl Calleman, *The Nine Waves of Creation*

> "Within each one of us lies dormant abilities and extraordinary potentials far beyond what was believed possible in the past. New discoveries ranging from human evolution and genetics to the emerging science of neuro-cardiology and heart intelligence have now overturned 150 years of thinking when it comes to who we are, and what we're capable of...we've the technology we have been waiting for."
> – Gregg Braden

> "Since the dawn of civilization, the idea of Heaven on Earth has been one of humanity's muse—inspiring and luring us home to a new possibility...most of the 7.9 billion human beings are worried about...where we may end up if we continue on our current trajectory. Fortunately, evolution has something else in mind...there

are waves of evolution that have creational forces, activations and patterns that bring forth new potentials. As human beings, we can begin to access the kind of unity that moves us beyond our separateness, beyond light and dark, creating an entirely new operating system…

– Patricia Albere, *Evolutionary Collective; Mutual Awakenings*

"…evolution always proceeds by way of extreme crises that force the birth of a new species. We are in that savage process now and need to become spacious enough to contain within our consciousness two things we have never fully imagined before…a literal mutation of the human species will be influenced by three factors: 1) an unimaginably painful initiatory ordeal produced by the collapse of ecosystems and the collapse of industrial civilization itself resulting from pandemics and economic and ecological devastation. 2) An unwavering alignment with the birthing field in which humans really do…allow everything to be taken away from them except truth. 3) Radical service to the birth through rigorous spiritual practices and Sacred Activism in the context of nothing less than a planetary hospice situation."

– Andrew Harvey and Carolyn Baker, *Radical Regeneration*

"Unlocking your Quantum Powers to expand time, to experience "sustained fire" to keep you operating at your highest energy level; power to partner with the energy of the Universe, to expand and express your creativity without sacrificing your daily responsibilities, and to attract money, people, and resources you need to move your projects forward and achieve the level of success you're striving for."

– Jean Houston

"I'm pointing to authentic spiritual awakening in which the ego has been radically overridden by the Ultimate Principle, by the creative force of the cosmos, by what the Buddha called 'the roar of the timeless beyond.' It's a life in which our endless quest for self-fulfillment has been replaced by a passion to give our heart and soul to the awakening and upliftment of all of life, to bringing the Sacred into manifestation in this world. In this ultimate sub-mission to and alignment with the Absolute, the human being be-comes a living, breathing force for higher evolution. And this changes our relationship to being alive in unimaginable ways…If we want our life to change that profoundly, we have to come to terms with what we're doing here. That means cultivating a clear and unwavering intention to bring our life into alignment with [a] higher order. Cultivating this kind of intention requires a 24/7 commitment."

– Craig Hamilton, Founder, Integral Enlightenment

So fasten your seat belts and get ready for the ride of your life! I'll be with you every step of the way.

With love and gold light blessings,
Lauren O. Thyme
March 4, 2021

WHO IS LAUREN O. THYME?

At the tender age of five, Lauren experienced a near-death experience. When she came out of her coma, she could then see and hear her Council of Elders (a group of Ascended Masters who advise, teach and nurture her) and became clairvoyant, clairsentient, clairaudient, mediumistic, and pre-cognitive. Lauren remembers 105 of her past lives in detail, including identifying people she meets and what their relationship have been in one or more past lives. She remembers her lifetime in Lemuria since she was 15 years old.

Her Amazon/Kindle book, *Traveling on the River of Time,* is a self-help book for you to explore your own past lives.

She has published 14 books which are sold world-wide and is a contributor to the anthology **Awaken The Feminine!** *FATE* magazine published her article: "My Life with Fairies and Devas," while her articles on sacred sites came out in *Power Places* magazine and *Magickal Blend.*

Lauren O. Thyme has been a psychic and spiritual counselor for the last 55 years. She has also been a professional astrologer for 46 years. Ms. Thyme graduated with a B.S. in Psychology from Sierra University in 1988 and studied with Dr. Joshua David Stone for a year's internship in order to become a MFC counselor.

Lauren studied with Peter Paddon, High Priest of Sekhmet, and was ordained as Priestess of Hathor through the Fellowship of Isis. Lauren created her own Egyptian Lyceum (school) of Hathor, Sekhmet, and Anubis, and continued her studies of ancient Egyptian Mystery School. She went on metaphysical tours to Egypt three times, the last time while leading her own metaphysical tour. Four of her past lifetimes included being an initiate, twice a Priestess, as well as a High Priestess of Hathor at Dendera, Egypt and she wrote *Along the Nile* as a result of her travels.

In 1996 Lauren had a major transformational experience and was gifted with a new birthday and birth chart. After that experience Lauren was drawn to travel internationally, visiting sacred sites while writing and publishing articles based on her experiences there. Her website, Time Travel. freely promoted metaphysical tours offered by 106 tour companies. She created The Egypt Store and sold Egyptian reproductions.

For 40 years Lauren has been an organic gardener and also owned/operated a permaculture farm for 7 years on Whidbey Island in Washington state. She has two children and two grandchildren and currently lives in Santa Fe, New Mexico.

WEBSITES and BLOGS

www.laurenothyme.com
www.thelemurianway.com

YOUTUBE VIDEOS:
Lauren Thyme — Here's first one: https://youtu.be/31TcK7Dgj5Y

LAUREN'S BLOG:
https://laurenothyme.com

TRANSLATIONS of *The Lemurian Way* are available in Dutch, German, French, Italian, Portuguese and Spanish.

TRANSLATIONS *of Living in the New Lemuria* will be out in Dutch, German, French, Italian, Portuguese and Spanish in 2021.

LIVING IN THE NEW LEMURIA:

EXERCISES, PRACTICES, AND TECHNIQUES

LIVING IN THE NEW LEMURIA:

EXERCISES, PRACTICES, AND TECHNIQUES

Class #1
Getting Started

Hello! Warm loving greetings and welcome to the first class of a series designed to assist you in using concepts from *The Lemurian Way, Remembering Your Essential Nature* in your life. I'm Lauren O. Thyme, author of *The Lemurian Way*.

In September 2020 when the Lemurian Elders woke me up from a deep sleep to ask me to teach a series of classes based on *The Lemurian Way*, I wholeheartedly said, "Yes!" I immediately started writing and teaching the classes that eventually became the foundation of this book.

The book *Living in the New Lemuria: exercises, practices and techniques* is based on Classes 1 through 12 from *Living in the New Lemuria: Exercises, Practices and Techniques,* originally offered as interactive classes on Zoom.

Lauren's Law #4: "Be aware. Transformation just ahead."

Contained within this book are lectures, explanations, quotes, essays, along with Lauren's Laws from *Cosmic Grandma Wisdom*. Included are simple yet powerful exercises to help you embody, deepen and transform yourself using

Gold Light Wisdom and other Lemurian (spiritual) principles. If you like, you can consider yourself to be a Lemurian Elder-in-training.

During the classes, you will have an opportunity to practice exercises and read information that the Lemurian Elders want to share with you. At the end of each class, you will finish with a meditation located energetically at Mt. Shasta, a holy mountain in northern California that is one of the remaining locations of Lemuria.

Obtain a notebook so that you can make notes, do exercises and complete homework assignments.

Notebook: Set aside a special time each day to write your observations, feelings and thoughts. Taking notes engages the kinesthetic (physical/feeling) part of your perception and literally bonds what you write into the cells of your body. Reviewing your notes later is a helpful way to gauge your progress. Keeping notes helps to review what you've learned.

Other items you will need are:

- A container such as a large jar, box, tin, or hatbox which you will label Creator Source;

- Something to write with such as a pen or pencil;

- 8 yards of yellow or gold yarn;

- A tape recorder or a cellphone to make recordings of exercises you want to practice.

Preparation for Classes

- Take an 8.5" x 11" piece of paper, cut it into 10 slips and have those available

- .Have a pen or pencil handy.

- Have your Creator Source Container handy.

- Have your notebook handy.

- Have a tape recorder or cell phone handy to record exercises if you wish.

There are infinite degrees and stages of learning in this book with exercises you can use to glean for answers. Ancient Lemurian Elders were born in apprenticeship, learning hands-on for 20-50 years. I have been learning from the Elders since age five, one step at a time for 68 years. What I teach will help you to accomplish this training relatively unscathed and it won't take you 20, 50 or 68 years!

FOUR STEPS OF LEARNING

You are not born knowing. You must learn the entirety of life from how to crawl, to understanding complicated concepts and procedures, through a process of acquiring and utilizing information. This learning follows the steps below, starting at unconscious incompetence and ending up with unconscious competence. You can remember these steps throughout this book and beyond as you gain knowledge and proficiency and advance yourself.

1) Unconscious Incompetence—When you don't know what you don't know.

Example: You rode with other people in their cars, but you didn't know what it takes to drive one.

2) Conscious Incompetence—When you begin to realize how little you know.

Example: You can sit in the car, perhaps even put the keys in the ignition and turn it on, maybe back out of the driveway, and practice on back streets. This stage requires extreme attention and cautiousness.

3) Conscious Competence

You are learning but you are not yet proficient. You have to pay attention and practice a lot.

Example: To drive you have to adjust the mirror, pay scrupulous attention to details, put the car into drive, look both ways carefully, ease out into traffic, etc.

4) Unconscious Competence

Without having to think about it, you know what to do. You have to focus and remember in order to teach someone else what you know.
Example: You get into your car, start it and drive away.

Lauren's Law #5: M = ET²

Miracles/Matter/Manifestation/ & Time —-Equals - Energized Thought — Squared —(of **Two** or more people)

Although it is not necessary, doing this work as a group is the Lemurian Way and speeds up the process. You may consider asking a friend or two to do the book with you.

Lauren's Law #24: "Pay attention as if your life depends on it. It does."

Developing one's own discernment takes time while "paying attention" to messages, events and experiences, and then following where they lead you. Discernment works through feeling in the body. Without feeling it is only knowledge and information without physical connection.

Lauren's Law #13: "The Universe is all about timing. So is everything in your life."

You can speed up or slow down participating in these exercises as you like. If you wish to spend more or less time practicing any given exercise, feel free to do so, even repeating them as desired. You may not find instant, easy answers, while paying assiduous attention to details, getting messages for yourself, trusting them and practicing, practicing, practicing. Be patient with the process and yourself. This course is taking you where you intend to go.

There is a slogan from 12-step groups that is relevant to remember here: "Progress, not Perfection."

The Elders and I proceed in an orderly fashion, one lesson building on another. Most everything in this book is a process of building a foundation piece by piece - learning discernment, finding information from inside yourself, and doing the exercises. Answers come as part of the emerging whole. Exercises may seem like kindergarten work, even tedious. One might wish for a magic wand. These exercises are powerful while seeming to be simplistic. Think of them as building blocks, tinker toys for the soul.

I am in process of creating YouTube videos of many exercises in this book including the Mt. Shasta meditation. To find them, you can google YouTube *Living in the New Lemuria* or my name Lauren Thyme.

***

The lessons are based on my book, *The Lemurian Way, Remembering Your Essential Nature*, as well as 40 years of on-going material that the Lemurian Elders continue to share with me. If you don't have the book, you can buy one from Kindle or Amazon. If you would like an autographed copy, contact me at thyme.lauren@gmail.com (this offer is only available in the USA).

I have taught concepts to people who had consultations with me; otherwise, this is the first time many of these exercises and concepts are being presented. These are intended to stimulate your spiritual transformation.

I often refer to Dr. Carl Calleman's book *The Nine Waves of Creation* which details the exquisite timing of the Mayan calendar as it relates to our consciousness. Dr. Calleman has studied the Mayan calendar for decades. He conveys an incisive, in-depth examination of the top five waves of creation which affect all people on this planet, most importantly the Ninth Wave.

THE NEW LEMURIAN

The New Lemurian is a highly spiritual person desiring harmony, unity, peaceful co-existence, non-judgment of others, fundamental connection to Creator Source and a willingness to develop values at a profound, responsive, and grounded level. I welcome you to become a New Lemurian.

To yearn to become a New Lemurian is a stimulating and exciting concept while to study the Lemurian Way is an essential component to grow into what the original Lemurians were born into.

A soul coming into ancient Lemurian life was pre-programmed in different ways:

— The soul was contacted by the Elders, who also consulted the heavens for information. The person was chosen for the "job" he or she would perform on behalf of their friends and neighbors as well as themselves.

— Selection of genes was precise as written in *The Lemurian Way* by strict selection of mother and father.

— The soul was welcomed into the community. For 20, 30 or more years the soul was raised in loving arms of the community and taught to perform the job they were coming in to perfect by masters of that profession.

— The original Lemurians didn't have the limitation of a strictly physical body which would break down and die within a century or so, nor did they have the constraint of a mental (ego) body which would give conflicting information not necessarily aligned with Creator Source.

— The Elders were on hand to consult with and to be loving guides for all those in their communities.

Finally, a soul had thousands of leisurely years to perfect themself, not needing to earn a living while working in a spiritual team for the betterment of all.

***

My first lifetime on earth was in Lemuria. The Lemurian Elders have been working with me in this life since I was 5 years old. When I was 15, I started remembering details of my Lemurian life. By the time I was 17 I was undertaking spiritual consultations for others. Since then, for 47 years, I've been doing spiritual, psychic, past lives, and astrological consultations, along with teaching and lecturing. I currently have 11 books in print with spiritual, metaphysical, and healing themes, and now present this new series of classes in book form.

***

Notebook: Get out your notebook and turn to the first page. Answer the following questions.

Now that you know who I am, tell me who you are.
What is your name?
What country are you living in?
Have you read *The Lemurian Way? Yes or no*
What do you hope to gain from these classes?

***

During these tumultuous and transformative times these teachings can be invaluable in your life because you'll develop a sense of peace and refuge from the turmoil. Not only are they valuable for you personally these classes are also designed to help teachers, counselors, psychologists and shamans who have decided to take this course to fulfill their missions as clearly and compassionately as possible. I envision these classes will bring peace and renewal, while supporting conscious evolution, unity and co-creation.

I believe we decide as a soul in our *life between lives* what we want to do, learn and heal. An astrology chart is created for us by us while our spiritual guides help us with the choices which we are born with. A chart is a blueprint of our skills, talents, proclivities, challenges, health and even our relationships.

Lauren's Law #32: "Challenges are required, like rainwater, in order to learn and grow."

Accordingly, many of us who chose to incarnate on Earth at this especially challenging time are clear about what we came here to do:

1   Observe the challenges of Earth - its land, water, air, animals, mammals, birds, amphibians, fish, and people, then ask "How can I help? Where am I most needed?"

2   Be of service to all who need us.

3   Be strong and resilient.

4   Be loving, peaceful, kind, helpful, and compassionate (all examples of Lemurian Gold Light Wisdom).

5   Practice higher knowledge to become the best selves we can be.

6   Heal our own karma and other lifetimes while being in service.

Lauren's Law #16: "Instant Karma –
Karma can be quick depending on your awareness, for the purpose of instant learning. The more you learn, the more aware you become, the faster your karma heals. It is a self-reinforcing loop."

Lauren's Law #17: "Grace trumps Karma."
Grace includes many concepts from Gold Light Wisdom,
which you will be learning and practicing in this book.

***

HISTORY

Lemuria existed approximately 105,000 years ago on a huge continent in the Pacific Ocean, during the Mayan 5th Wave. To date, Lemuria is the most spiritual civilization to exist on the planet. During that time, there was no duality, no hierarchy, and all people felt harmoniously connected. Due to massive tectonic activity, including earthquakes and volcanoes, most of Lemuria is now submerged.

Earth was originally created as a playground, a kind of enormous Disney World, with its beauty, flora and fauna with engaging physical sensations and five senses. In the intervening years, as humans became enmeshed in the 3rd dimension, forgetting our missions, Earth stopped being "fun." Since 2011 we have the opportunity to regain Earth's former status.

Beginning March 9, 2011, we entered the 9th and final wave of creation, according to the Mayan calendar as interpreted by Dr. Carl Calleman in his book, *The Nine Waves of Creation*[1], bringing in non-duality, while planetary unity, conscious co-creation, and a conscious connection with the Divine prevails, what the Lemurians called Creator Source. The essence of Lemuria is available to us and pulsing with energy via the 9th wave.

Unfortunately, the 6th, 7th, and 8th waves of creation are also functioning and will continue into infinity. The 6th wave, which is interfering with the 9th wave, has a long history of 5135 years of planetary consciousness, including what Dr. Calleman calls the *Hologram of Good and Evil*. The 6th wave, which commenced 3115 BCE, introduced creation of civilization for the first time in human history. The 6th wave brought in a focus on left brain activity and the masculine, duality, hierarchy, and separation not only from our planet, but also from each other, which is currently seen worldwide in polarity consciousness.

My desire is to help you anchor the 9th wave of unity, conscious co-creation and connection with Creator Source using *The Lemurian Way* as a guide in these Lemurian classes.

Lauren's Law #20: "Everything is connected to everything as though by an immense Spider Web of Life."

A change will vibrate the entire web; thus, ONE person CAN make a difference. (Quantum physicists and string theorists seem to be in agreement with me on this.)

"For [David] Bohm, whom Einstein called 'my spiritual son' and the Dalai Lama called his 'science guru,' life included nature and consciousness in one single wholeness. At a deeper, quantum level, everything is interconnected and internally related to everything else, *each part of the cosmos contains the whole universe.*" From the video "Infinite Potential."*

The Lemurian Way, the manner which Lemurians conducted their lives spiritually, with deep compassionate love, is based on Gold Light Wisdom embracing many concepts including unconditional love of self and others, surrender to a higher power, blamelessness, defenselessness, compassion, mutual acceptance and forgiveness. The more you practice the pieces of Gold Light Wisdom, the more your life will come into harmony and you will feel peace with All There Is.

I will share these and many other concepts with you and offer exercises to incorporate them into your life in a tangible way. What I teach is simple and can be practiced anytime and anywhere.

***

GOLD LIGHT WISDOM MANTRA — EXERCISE #1

The first exercise of this book is a mantra based on the Lemurian Pieces of Gold Light Wisdom from *The Lemurian Way*.

Say aloud each word or phrase. After saying each one you will take a breath.

I now have:
—Unconditional love of self and others
—Acceptance and allowing
—Blamelessness
—Willingness
—Noticing without criticism
—Forgiveness of self and others
—Patience
—Mutual respect
—Mutual support
—Detachment
—Living in present time
—Open and loving communication
—Trust in and surrender to a higher power
—Gratitude
—Defenselessness and neutrality
—Giving and receiving
—Joyful creation
—Feeling my emotions
—Empathy and compassion
—Psychic abilities and telepathy

—Having fun
—Doing what I love
—Loving what I do
—Unity
—Harmony
—Peace

(Excerpt from *The Lemurian Way* © 2000)

You can focus on one of these attributes every day.

You can print out this list and attach it where you can easily see it every day such as your refrigerator or your bathroom mirror.

***

SURRENDERING TO CREATOR SOURCE — EXERCISE #2

The Lemurian Elders taught me a magnificent mantra that I live by and now share with you: *"Everything is perfect, no matter what it looks like, for the purpose of learning, growth and evolution."*

This means that regardless of what is going on in your life or around the planet, all events including your life, are part of a Divine Plan for us to learn, grow and evolve as individuals and as a group. Sometimes we may feel upset as the Divine Plan may not meet our hopes, wishes and expectations. Using this mantra is a way of gently aligning with Creator Source. To use this mantra when upset is a practice of surrendering to Creator Source and thus to the Divine Plan.

"Let go and let God." —- 12-Step program spiritual slogan

"Made a decision to turn our will and lives over to the care of God as we understood God." —- Step 3 of the Al-Anon 12-Step program

"…The 9th wave [analogous to concepts in *The Lemurian Way*] … helps us to see the unity of all things and how everything is connected. To the extent that we surrender to the Divine…our individual destinies will also become part of the overall collective destiny of humanity." —- Carl Calleman, *The Nine Waves of Creation*

Lauren's Law #30: "Never give up – just surrender. Expect nothing (surrender) and expect a miracle (surrender). Simply surrender and let the Universe take care of the juice of life."

Surrender is not about giving up, rather that you are aligning with the energy of the Divine.

Why don't you try it now?

Steps:

Relax in your chair. Think of something currently bothering you such as a person, a feeling, or incident.

Now say the following phrase out loud while focusing on your distress:

"Everything is perfect, no matter what it looks like, for the purpose of learning, growth and evolution."

Repeat: "Everything is perfect, no matter what it looks like, for the purpose of learning, growth and evolution."

And yet again: "Everything is perfect, no matter what it looks like, for the purpose of learning, growth and evolution."

Visualize and feel the distress evaporating because of this new insight.

To become proficient at surrendering, this exercise requires practice, which you can do any time day or night, wherever you may be.

Notebook: You can write these phrases 10 times in your notebook. You can also attach sticky notes around your home with each powerful, transformative phrase to remind yourself.

Next is the 2nd Surrender Exercise I invite you to practice, what I call the John Travolta Surrender Dance (from his famous disco scene in the movie *Saturday Night Fever*).

> First think of something uncomfortable. Imagine Creator Source to your Right and above you. Offer the discomfort with your right hand to Creator Source and say, "Here, God" or "Here, Goddess" or "Here, Universe" or whatever name you choose to call it. Imagine that Creator Source has now taken the discomfort off your hands.

> Next, imagine Creator Source to your Left and above you. Offer the discomfort with your left hand to Creator Source and say, "Here, God," "Here, Goddess," "Here, Universe" or whatever name you choose to call it. Imagine that Creator Source has now taken the discomfort off your hands again.

> Finally, imagine Creator Source has completely removed your discomfort when you say the words "I'm stayin' alive." **

As you practice this, you may also receive a message to do something else, like call a friend for support or take some specific action. The message may also include a follow up exercise. During the course I will introduce many exercises you can utilize.

Notebook: In your notebook write down your experience of these two Surrender exercises.

Practice.

***

SACRED BECOMING RITUAL MEDITATION using GOLD LIGHT – EXERCISE #3

Gold Light Wisdom includes Unconditional Love of self and others, along with Unity and Connectedness.

The next ritual is intended for you to become joined to Lemurians (spiritual people), the way it originally was practiced in Lemuria, using Unity, Harmony, Connecting with Others, while connecting to and transforming with Gold Light.

Gold Light is the most powerful, transformational light in the Universe.

When a child was born into Lemuria, she or he was united with all others in local and global communities to experience unconditional love of self and others through the Sacred Becoming Ritual using Gold Light.

Record: You may find it convenient to record the words of the following ritual so you can listen to it any time you want. This exercise is also recorded on YouTube under "Sacred Becoming Ritual."

I will now guide you through your own Sacred Becoming Ritual.

Steps:

Make sure you won't be disturbed for 15 minutes. Make yourself comfortable.

Close your eyes and take a deep breath. Relax into your body. Imagine that you are lying on a clearing of soft sweet grass with lush foliage all around. The bright green leaves shimmer in the sunlight. You can hear birds singing in the trees. The azure sky above you is awash with cotton candy clouds. You feel warm, comforted and safely embraced by nature.

Take another deep breath and exhale. Sigh if you need to. Breathe into your solar plexus and pull the breath up into your heart like an ocean of love, and exhale.

In the distance you can hear the sounds of a waterfall gurgling over rocks down to a clear pool at the bottom.

As you take another breath, the aroma of fragrant flowers tickles your nose. They smell perfumed and familiar. You hear the sound of drums and flutes gently wafting in the breeze. You become aware that the sound is slowly moving towards you. The music fills you with joy and recognition. It's your Lemurian brothers and sisters coming to visit you. You clearly hear their melodious voices singing a harmonious song, one that you had forgotten but now remember.

As you lie in the clearing, eyes closed, breathing calmly, you feel them approach quietly and gently, serenely singing their song to you. They form a circle around you. One of the people places a beautifully faceted crystal on your solar plexus, deepening your connection to the group.

You open your eyes and observe them performing a slow delicate whirling dance, and you begin to feel lighter and happier than you have ever known before. As they sing and dance around you, you notice that each body is filled with and surrounded by a dazzling yet tranquil golden light. The light from each body extends to all the others until you are surrounded by and floating in their warm golden glow.

A vortex of Gold Light Energy swirls, encircling you and your group with powerful emanations. The top of your head pulsates, and you sense a spiral of gold light enter your head from above. Your feet tingle, connecting you with the earth beneath you. Each of your sacred centers – the top of your head, center of your forehead, throat, heart, solar plexus, lower abdomen, genitals, and base of your spine begin to vibrate, glow and swirl like pinwheels of light.

The pinwheels swirl faster and glow brighter and you become even more aware of the motion in your body. You feel your body connected to the Earth beneath you and to the stars in the heavens above you. You sigh in contentment.

You feel the Gold Light of joy, harmony, and oneness bathe your glands and organs. Engulf your brain. Circulate in your blood. Fuse into your bones and flesh. Each of your individual cells is glowing and pulsing with Gold Light. You feel all problems melt away in the warmth of the Gold Light. You feel and see the connection of the Gold Light above you, your crystalline light body, and those of your family, singing and dancing around you… the Oneness of All.

You sense your cellular structure transforming, along with your DNA, becoming more of who you are. You are becoming the person you've always known you were meant to be: brighter, happier, content and at peace.

You are filled with excitement because now you are Home. Welcome home!

Take a deep, slow breath and exhale. Relax. Open your eyes. Feel your feet on the floor and your body seated in your chair. Stretch and come back to present time. Take one more deep breath all the way in, breathe out slowly until all the air is exhaled.

Notebook: Take out your notebook and write down your experience, any impressions you had, who may have joined you in this exercise (like family and friends including those who are deceased) and how you feel.

***

LAUREN'S LAWS

These "LAWS" are based on my 73 years of observation, learning, experimenting, trial and error. You don't have to "believe" in any of them. I will be referring to these Laws throughout this book. The LAWS are presented here for contemplation.

1. **"We each live in our own separate Universe."** Everything in that universe is true and correct for that universe. There is no truth with a capital T, no reality with a capital R.

2. **"Love is the building block of the universe, from which everything emanates."** It's in you, around you, it IS you. If you cannot feel love right now, don't worry. It's still there.

3. **"If it's easy, it's right."** If a project is or becomes difficult, stop. You might be going the wrong direction, using the wrong tools, being in the wrong time or place, beating your head against a brick wall. Wait for clarity. Or simply take some time out.

4. **"Be aware. Transformation just ahead."**

5. $M = ET^2$
   Miracles/Matter/Manifestation/ & Time =- Equals
   Energized Thought Squared —- (of **Two** or more people)

   Miracles, physical matter, manifestations, events, space, and/or time can be speeded up, increased or transformed through the elevated (spiritual) interaction of two or more people. One person plus one person equals more than two people. Two people plus two people equals MUCH more than four people. The increase of energy is exponential.

6. **"I can unconditionally love someone, but do not have to go to dinner with him or her."**

7. **"A relationship lasts as long as it lasts – not one minute longer. And you'll know the moment the relationship has ended."**

8. **"When a relationship comes to an end, bless it and move on."** There's no turning back once that lesson is learned.

9. **"Relationships are like buses."** There's always the next one to catch to take you to a new destination.

10. **"When a difficult person arrives in your life, love that person, forgive and be grateful."** The universe has sent that person to you as a gift for your learning.

11. **"When a difficult situation arrives in your life, love that situation, forgive and be grateful."** The universe has sent that situation to you as a gift for your learning.

12. **"When you need something, give."**

13. **"The universe is all about timing. So is everything in your life."**

14. **"There is no one to blame."**

15. **"Ended relationships are not failures."** Once you are finished learning with a person, you are on to the next (it might be yourself) for the purpose of personal learning, growing and evolving.

16. **"Instant Karma."** Karma can be quick depending on your awareness, for the purpose of instant learning. The more you learn, the more aware you become, the faster karma works. It is a self-reinforcing loop.

17. **"Grace trumps Karma."**

18. **"Tell the truth......as fast as you can."** This may not mean immediately. Sometimes appropriate timing is involved. Truth opens up all kinds of avenues that may not have been open before. Tell the truth with compassion and kindness.

19. **"There is no such thing as a lie, not even a 'little white lie.'"** This includes telling outright falsehoods as well as failing to tell the truth. Lies cannot and do not exist. Everyone is psychic. Everyone intuits another's emotions and intentions and behaves according to that intuition, even if the intuition is unconscious. Attempting to lie (or failing to tell the truth) will create problems for everyone including oneself. Many of today's world problems are based on attempts to lie. Many movies are based on the interaction around a falsehood. That kind of movie plot couldn't exist without an attempt to conceal, hide, avoid, or run from the truth; the movie would be over in a matter of minutes had the truth been told at the beginning.

20. **"Everything is connected to everything as though by an immense Spider Web of Life."** A change will vibrate the entire web; thus, ONE person CAN make a difference. (Quantum physicists and string theorists seem to be in agreement with me.)

21. "Everything is perfect, no matter what it looks like, for the purpose of growing, learning and evolving."

22. "Everything is perfect, no matter whether it changes or not."

23. "Forgiveness is selfish – for your own peace, happiness and well-being."

24. "Pay attention as if your life depends on it. It does."

25. "Everyone is psychic."

26. "As I transform myself, other people transform themselves in my presence."

27. "The mind is not my friend."

28. "Grief is my friend, so I can feel how much I love."

29. "Accept everything."

30. "Never give up – just surrender. Expect nothing (surrender) and expect a miracle (surrender). Simply surrender and let the Universe take care of the juice of life."

31. "I belong to the Church of It's Good Enough."

32. "Challenges are required, like rainwater, in order to learn and grow."

Excerpt from Cosmic Grandma Wisdom © 2017   Lauren O. Thyme
Article first published in fatemagazine.com and galdepress.com © 8/15/2012

***

RITUAL GROUP MEDITATION: TRAVELING IN YOUR ETHERIC BODY TO MT. SHASTA - EXERCISE #4

Next you will attend a ritual group meditation traveling in your etheric body to Mt. Shasta, a Lemurian sacred place in northern California. You will be instructed to do this exercise at the end of every class. Every time you do this exercise you will grow and expand in ways you cannot comprehend at this moment.

Who is the Group in this meditation? When you experience this exercise, you most likely will see, hear and feel other people, those you know and those you don't. The word has gone out that there are regular group meditations at Mt. Shasta and Lemurians are showing up.

Years ago, I led a weekly group meditation to Mt. Shasta. We didn't go there in person; we traveled in our etheric soul bodies, which Lemurians are adept at doing. Mt. Shasta is a holy mountain, one of a few remnants of Lemuria. Some say Lemurians live inside that mountain.

This ritual contains an experience of group unity, another piece of Gold Light Wisdom, along with trust, telepathic training, compassion and empathy, at a Lemurian sacred place. Invite your friends!

There is no right or wrong way to do this exercise. Simply and gently open yourself up to whatever you experience – which will be perfect for you today. I encourage you to *make it up* if you're not certain. This means you are inviting your Higher Self to bring new experiences and all you have to do is be willing to receive – which is trust.

I will instruct you to do this practice after every class to deepen your experiences as you connect in unity with "others" at this sacred Lemurian place, profoundly training yourself in telepathy, compassion and empathy while traveling in your soul body as original Lemurians were capable of doing.

Record: You may find it convenient to record the words of the meditation so you can listen to it any time you want. This can be found at YouTube "Mt. Shasta meditation Exercise #4."

Timer: You will need a timer to time yourself for 5 minutes of silent meditation towards the end of this exercise.

Steps:

Get comfortable in your chair. Close your eyes and slowly take a deep breath and exhale. Do this three times.

Now take your logical mind and place it next to you. You won't need your logical mind for this exercise. You can pick it up when you're done.

Say to yourself, "I'm going to Mt. Shasta and I will meet other Lemurian friends there." Then relax even more.

Imagine that your spiritual body is journeying to Mt. Shasta. As you arrive, you notice there are other people there as well. I may also meet you there. You can greet them, smile, hug if you want to do so. Feel the unified feeling of oneness you are experiencing there with them. You may feel sensations: vibrating, and tingling in your heart area, on the top of your head, elsewhere in your body or other chakras. Some of what you feel may seem new or different to you. Relax. Everything is perfect.

Form a circle and join hands with the others. Feel other hands holding your hands. You may feel more sensations. You may have visuals of the people. You may hear talking. You may hear whispering or laughing. You may smell or taste impressions. Any and all of these sensations and experiences are normal. Trust. Be open to whatever comes to you. This is Creator Source's gift to you. Feel free to *make it up*.

Whatever you make up will be perfect for you. Imagination is part of and connected to your Higher Self.

This is your family. Discern individuals if you can. If not, *make them up*.

Suddenly you hear singing. You feel like dancing. So, go ahead. Sing. Dance. Your Lemurian family is there to play with you.

You may want to have a banquet with your new Lemurian friends, to celebrate your homecoming. Imagine a feast set out on beautiful tables with flowers. Taste the food. Share food with others. Imagine your delight and happiness. All this may take place quickly, even instantly. You and the others are in your soul bodies which are capable of anything at the speed of thought.

You see a person there who seems familiar to you. Go to that person now. Tell that person what you feel about him or her. Listen – is that person talking to you? What is that person saying?

Timer: Now set your timer for 5 minutes of silent meditation…

[**after 5 minutes**] …you realize it is time to return to your physical body in your separate home. You will remember this experience forever. After each class, you will end with this same ritual experience. You are now connected to these other Lemurians and they are connected to you. You are no longer alone. You are part of a growing community of people unified in love, peace and happiness, no longer separate, no longer lonely, no longer divisive. With every passing day, this unconditional love and unification grows in strength and numbers. You can pass on that love and unity to others, even if they didn't join you in this class. On this planet we are all connected as one heart.

In a flash you are back in your physical body in your physical home. With a deep breath and a lingering sigh, you thank yourself for your experience. You thank others who attended. You smile remembering your experiences. Now open your eyes and put your logical mind back in place. Feel your feet on the floor and your body seated in your chair. Stretch and come back to present time.

Notebook: Write down your experience, any impressions or messages you received, and people or beings who were there at Mt. Shasta with you. As more people do this meditation, "Lemurians" are showing up at Mt. Shasta to join with us.

You may discover that each time you do this Mt. Shasta meditation, you will have different experiences and "meet" different people, while deepening your abilities.

***

If you have questions or concerns, you may send me an email at *thyme.lauren@gmail.com.*

Infinite Potential video on life and ideas of David Bohm   *https://www.infinitepotential.com/watch/*

**Words from the BeeGees

[1] *The Nine Waves of Creation*, Dr. Carl Calleman © 2016

[2] *Cosmic Grandma Wisdom*, Lauren O. Thyme © 2017

The Lemurian Way, Remembering Your Essential Nature, Lauren O. Thyme © 2000

Journey of Souls: The Life between Lives, Dr. Michael Newton © 1994

LIVING IN THE NEW LEMURIA:

EXERCISES, PRACTICES, AND TECHNIQUES

Class #2
Unity, Unconditional Love, Acceptance, Surrender and Willingness

Many of us watched with concern as various events unfolded during 2020.

> *"Everything is perfect, no matter what it looks like,*
> *for the purpose of learning, growth and evolution."*

In Lemuria everyone knew that each person had meaning and was valuable and important to the whole. They also knew that an individual's consciousness affects the consciousness of the group. The Elders taught them, *"We all inhabit a spider web of existence. One person can vibrate the web thus affecting the whole."*

> **Lauren's Law #26: "As I transform myself,**
> **others transform themselves in my presence."**

"In my presence" can mean directly **next** to you or dynamically **across** the planet from you.

I bless people on our beloved planet regularly as a Lemurian practice of peace, harmony, and unity, focusing on the Gold Light Wisdom of unconditional love, mutual respect, acceptance, surrender, and willingness. If I don't bless, then I risk running the gamut from judgment, disgust, and resentment, all the way to hatred, even violence. *I would then be part of the problem, not the solution.* I prefer to be part of the solution. I have had decades of experience blessing and forgiving people who are challenging. I thank Liah Holtzman for her wise counsel as we co-authored the book *Forgiveness Equals Fortune*[2] available on Amazon.

The Lemurian practice of unity and interconnectedness grows in strength and harmony the more often it is practiced.

I will explore some of these Gold Light Wisdom elements in a Lemurian exercise that the Elders have recently and quite insistently shared with me. This Lemurian blessing practice that you will do next leads to feelings of liberation from negativity and judgment. Don't be deceived by the simplicity of this exercise. It is powerful.

You may wish to keep your eyes open for the following exercise. This exercise is particularly potent when performed during a solstice, equinox, eclipse, new moon or full moon.

You may find this blessing exercise to be challenging; however, the power that accrues from practicing these blessings leads to peace of mind, serenity, and tranquility for you and those around you. You may even become more fun to be with!!

Make sure you are in a space that allows you to be uninterrupted for 30 minutes or so. Cut 10 strips of paper and have a pen or pencil handy. Have your Creator Source Container close at hand. Then sit comfortably at your computer, tablet, or laptop and focus on the directions.

Take a deep breath and slowly exhale. Relax.

LEMURIAN BLESSING EXERCISE # 5

Steps:

Imagine that Creator Source is floating above you in a giant warm bubble of gold light like the sun. You may have your own favorite name for this Higher Power, such as God, Goddess, Jesus, Shiva, Buddha, Allah, or the Divine. Whatever your chosen name is, focus on Creator Source right now.

Gold Light was used by the Lemurians for all their sacred rituals and is the most powerful light in the universe for transformation. Ask Creator Source to send Gold Light Blessings into your body through the top of your head. Feel the gold light warmth and peaceful flow as it enters your body. Allow it to radiate throughout your head, into your body, arms, legs and feet, then into the ground below you. Deeply breathe again and feel the blessings you are receiving from Creator Source. You feel ever more relaxed and receptive.

When you are ready, think of five people who are beloved and special to you. An individual may be living or deceased. You may include a special pet as one of the five "beloveds." You can always add other individuals to your Container at a later time. Right now, I want you to focus on just five. Write each person's name on its own slip of paper and place it lovingly in the Container.

When you have placed all five names in the Container, put your hand over the top of it and ask Creator Source to bless each of these persons with Gold Light. Ask Creator Source aloud for this blessing, speaking each of the names on the slips. Do this now.

Feel the blessing emanating to each individual. You may see the Gold Light entering each person. You may smell flowers or fragrances arising from the blessing. You may intuitively taste a special food that you associate with a certain individual. You may hear music that you associate with that person. Take your time in this process. Linger in the blessings each person receives. You may experience joy that you can share Creator Source's blessing with each person.

Now remove your hand from the Container and let go of the five people, knowing that they have been blessed by an infinitely loving Source.

Now you will go into an even deeper level practicing unity, harmony, and blessings in an entirely new way, using willingness and acceptance, both highly elevated states of spiritual being.

Take a deep breath and focus on the Gold Light still streaming into your head and body from Creator Source. Say the following words aloud, "I accept. I am willing…" Willingness and acceptance is an illuminating spiritual part of wisdom with great power to heal both yourself and the planet. Feel acceptance and willingness enter your body from Creator Source, filling you with a blissful, peaceful knowing, as the Gold Light imbues you.

Take another deep breath, gently exhale, and relax. You may say aloud, "Everything is perfect, no matter what it looks like, for the purpose of learning, growth and evolution."

Now I want you to think of an individual, living or dead, with whom you DO not or DID not have harmonious feelings or relationship. Write the name of that individual on a slip of paper and place it gently into the Container. Put your hand over the top of the Container. "Creator Source bless this person" pronouncing his or her name aloud. Do this now.

See, hear, feel, smell and taste the blessing that radiates to the Creator Source Container, knowing that you are creating a space of peace and acceptance between that person and you. If you have difficulty with this, you may say aloud, "Creator Source, I am **willing** to bless _____ (insert the person's name here)."

Understand that blessing or forgiving does not exempt that person from consequences for actions they may have committed. It **does** mean you are willing to free yourself from the tyranny of judgment.

If you need to, take a deep breath and relax even more deeply. Repeat, "I am **willing** to bless this person." Or if you are ready, you can say, "I bless _____ now (name the person). I ask for all good things to flow from Creator Source into this person." Do this now.

Take a deep breath and feel your body relax.

While requesting this blessing with your hand over the Container, sense the space you are creating on the planet – for peace, harmony and unity. Do this now.

Now I want you to think of a second individual, living or dead, with whom you do not or did not have harmonious feelings or relationship.

Write that person's name on a slip of paper and place it gently into the Container. Put your hand over the top of the Container. Say, "Creator Source, bless ___ (say this person's name) now."

See, hear, feel, smell and taste the blessing that radiates to the Container from Creator Source, knowing that you are creating a space of peace and acceptance between that person and you. If you have difficulty with this, say aloud, "Creator Source, I am **willing** to bless this person." You may also say aloud, *"Everything is perfect, no matter what it looks like, for the purpose of learning, growth and evolution."*

Understand that blessing or forgiving does not exempt that person from consequences for actions they may have committed. It does mean you are willing to free yourself from the tyranny of judgment.

If you need to, take a breath. Repeat. "I am **willing** to bless this person." Or if you are now ready, you can say, "I *bless* __ (name this person) now. I ask for all good things to flow from Creator Source to this person." Do this now. While requesting this blessing with your hand over the Container, sense the space you are creating on the planet – for peace, harmony and unity.

For the next segment of this contemplation, I ask you to focus on the Coronavirus. How do you feel or think about the Coronavirus? For months the Coronavirus has been seen by all of us as a fearsome or hated entity. Some of us may have lost loved ones, jobs, businesses, homes, or peace of mind to this virus. This may be a difficult blessing for the reasons mentioned above and others unspoken. Know that once you fulfill this practice, you may notice a sense of liberation and acceptance. Understand that this is a powerful blessing to perform.

Write the name **Coronavirus** or **Covid-19** on a slip of paper and place it gently into the Container. Put your hand over the top of the Container. Ask Creator Source, "Bless this virus *now.*" You may also say aloud, *"Everything is perfect, no matter what it looks like, for the purpose of learning, growth and evolution."*

See, hear, feel, smell and taste the blessing that radiates to the bowl from Creator Source, knowing that you are creating a space of peace, healing, and acceptance in yourself and on the planet. If you have difficulty with this, you may say aloud, "Creator Source, I am **willing** to bless this virus."

If you need to, take a deep breath to relax even more deeply. Repeat, "I am **willing** to bless this Coronavirus."

Or if you are now ready, you can say, "I bless this virus now. The virus is a gift to the planet, and I bless it. I am willing to know the perfection of this virus." You may say aloud, "*Everything is perfect, no matter what it looks like, for the purpose of learning, growth and evolution.*"

As you ask for this blessing with your hand over the Container, sense the space you are creating on the planet – for peace, harmony, healing, and unity.

For the final segment of this contemplation, I want you to think of a group of people that you have negative judgments about. These could include law enforcement officers, protestors, looters, government officials or any group you may have difficulty blessing.

Write the name of the group on a slip of paper then place it gently into the Container. Put your hand over the top of the Container. Ask Creator Source: "Bless this group of _____ (name group) now."

Understand that blessing or forgiving does *not* exempt that group from consequences for actions they may have committed. It *does* mean you are willing to free yourself from the tyranny of judgment. See, hear, feel, smell and taste the blessing that radiates to the Container from Creator Source, knowing that you are creating a space of peace, healing, and acceptance in yourself and the planet. "*As I transform, other people transform themselves in my presence.*" If you have difficulty with this blessing, you may say aloud, "Creator Source, I am **willing** to bless this group." You may say aloud: *"Everything is perfect, no matter what it looks like, for the purpose of learning, growth and evolution."*

If you need to, take a breath to relax more deeply. Repeat. "I am **willing** to bless this group." Or if you are now ready, you can say, "I bless this group __ (name them) now. The group is a gift to the planet, and I bless them."

As you ask for this final blessing with your hand over the Container, sense the space you are creating on the planet – for peace, harmony, healing, and unity.

Take a slow breath, release, and relax.

Thank Creator Source and yourself for the gifts and for the vitally important work you have done today.

Feel free to repeat this Lemurian blessing exercise as often as you wish for various individuals, groups or institutions. You can do this exercise as often as you wish, including yourself and other people you wish to bless. Feel free to share this with your friends and family. As more people do this, more blessings of peace are bestowed.

This blessing exercise was downloaded to Lauren on June 21, 2020 during a potent solar eclipse that occurred on the summer solstice.

Notebook: Journal your experience of this exercise. The YouTube Video of this exercise can be found at YouTube "Lemurian Blessing Exercise #5."

RITUAL GROUP MEDITATION TRAVELING
IN YOUR ETHERIC BODY
TO MT. SHASTA — EXERCISE #4

This is the time you can practice attending the ritual group meditation as you did at the end of Class #1. Although you may want to skip this exercise, I encourage you to repeat it often, as it will potentiate your growth.

Tape recorder or cellphone: You can use a tape recorder or a cellphone to make a recording of the original exercise to or go to YouTube to listen.

Notebook: Journal your experiences when finished.

***

The Hundredth Monkey, Ken Keyes, Jr. © 1984

Cosmic Grandma Wisdom, Lauren O. Thyme © 2017

The Lemurian Way, Remembering Your Essential Nature, Lauren O. Thyme © 2000

[1] *The Nine Waves of Creation,* Dr. Carl Calleman © 2016

[2] *Forgiveness equals Fortune*, 2nd edition, Liah Holtzman and Lauren O. Thyme © 2017

LIVING IN THE NEW LEMURIA:

EXERCISES, PRACTICES, AND TECHNIQUES

Class #3
Exploring Lemuria from Within

I've been asked by a number of people if they lived in Lemuria. If they did, what were their jobs? What kind of work did they plan to do here in this current life? Are they doing that work today?

With that in mind, I have an exciting exercise to share with you. This set of exercises will take you on a journey, using the past lives format I created for clients, then expanded upon in my book *Traveling on the River of Time.* You will get to see, feel, know and understand from the perspective of your Higher Self, the Lemurian you were and want to be again. This process is easy, painless and will, ideally, answer many questions. This process is also intended to take you to new and wonderful feelings for your New Lemurian self and a deeper expression of Lemurian experience.

I will ask you to make it up during this exercise. That is because during the Fifth wave of Lemuria 105,000 years BCE, we did not yet have the logical minds that we do today. We were easily connected to each other and Creator Source through our intuition and imagination. The logical mind did not get fully generated in the universe until the 6th Wave which started 3115 BCE. As much as you might enjoy your logical mind, it has limitations of judging, considering, deciding, assessing, and censoring. Thinking. Thinking. Thinking.

Lauren's Law #27: "The mind is not my friend."

Since the origination of the 9ᵗʰ Wave, which began in 2011, we do NOT need to focus on our logical mind, which is already strong enough, so we will put it aside during this exercise. Don't worry. You'll pick up your logical mind when you're done.

The reason for the next exercise is to activate any or all of the skills below:

- Limber up your intuition and spiritual "muscles by making it up, using your creative imagination.

- Discover who you were in Lemuria.

- Find information from within you and your Higher Self about what Lemuria felt and looked like.

- Discover the job you did while in Lemuria.

- Recognize people you knew in Lemuria who you know in this lifetime and what those relationships were and are.

- Find talents you didn't know about stemming from Lemuria and elsewhere.

- Understand vows, resolutions, oaths or decisions you made after being in your Lemurian lifetime that you brought forward with you.

- Remember your experiences, work and skills connected to your higher self.

The information you will receive is not merely interesting; it is vital for your life and work today, now that all of us on this planet are in the final 9th Wave of conscious co-creation. We are working to create a Golden Age, a Garden of Eden, a blissfully happy home on our planet.

Before you begin, you will start with your lifetime just prior to being born in this current life, in order for you to understand how to do the process before we move on to exploring your Lemurian lifetime. If you can't remember, don't worry. You will make it up.

Record: If you wish, you can record these steps on a cellphone or tape recorder. This exercise is on YouTube: "Living in the New Lemuria Exercise #6 Traveling on the River of Time."

Here are the Steps:
Prepare yourself to be receptive and contemplative. Allow yourself at least an hour without interruptions in a quiet, calm environment in order to be relaxed and serene, while you do this work. Your preparation can include meditation, a hot bath or a nap, to help you unwind, so that you can easily reach into the inner sanctum of your consciousness, to be guided by your Higher Self.

Keep your notebook at your side to make notes.

PAST LIVES - EXERCISE #6

- Set aside your logical mind. Imagine that you are pulling it off like a hat and putting it on a table next to you. You won't need it for this experience. You will be making it up as you go along. You cannot anticipate any exact answer as to what you will see, feel, hear, or sense on your voyage of discovery and you will have no way to prove or disprove what you uncover.

- Logic, rationality, and reasoning will be of no help nor necessary on this expedition. However, what you unearth will make profound sense to you and "feel" correct, plus you will be creating a valuable tool to gain information and learn how to trust your inner guidance, even if you have never done so before now.

- If you wish, you may close your eyes periodically in order to focus better.

- Imagine that your soul's vessel is moored on the River of Time.

- Get in and set sail or start the engine. If you like, you can bring a trusted friend, guide, counselor, teacher, or sage with you.

- You can pilot the boat or let someone else do it for you.

- Then begin traveling back along the River of Time.

- You will notice scenery around you. Take your time. Relax. You will see piers, docks, harbors, ports, anchorages, wharfs, and moorings.

- Continue to travel along the River until you find the place that was your most recent life. It may be a dock. It may be a clearing at the shore. If you are unsure where to stop, that's okay. You are learning to trust your intuition. If you are confused or hesitant, I encourage you to just make it up.

- "But what if I'm fantasizing?" you may ask. Imagining? Dreaming? Daydreaming? Those are links to your inner world and to your past lives. So, encourage yourself. You don't have to know for sure. You don't have to figure it out. Your logic is not important here. Only your experiences and your intuitions have meaning in this quest.

- When you find the mooring on the River of Time that represents your most recent past life, guide your boat there.

- Tie your boat at the dock, get out, and walk up the pier to your destination.

- At the end of the pier is a closed door.

- Open the door and walk through, closing it behind you.

WHO IS BEHIND THE DOOR?

- In front of you is a mirror. Look into it and examine the person that you see reflected there. It is you as you appeared in that lifetime.

- Are you male or female?

- What race are you?

- Are you old or young?

- What color is your hair?

- What color are your eyes?

- How are you dressed?

- What you are wearing will help in locating the period of time you find yourself in. Are you dressed well or poorly?

- Rags or expensive clothing? Your clothing (or lack of clothing) will determine the social/economic milieu you find yourself in and perhaps are a part of.

- Now ask yourself what country are you in?

- Can you determine this by how you're dressed? If you're unsure, make it up.

- Next to the mirror is a calendar. What is the month, day, and year? If you're undecided, make it up. A date will pop into your head.

- Ask yourself "what is my age?" If you don't know or can't decide, *make it up*. An answer will pop into your head.

THE 1ST IMPORTANT EVENT OF THAT LIFE

Go to the 1st important event of that life now.

- How old are you during this event?

- What are the circumstances of this event?

Use all your senses to experience it. Feel it, see it, hear, even smell what is happening.

- Can you hear any sounds?

- Are you with an individual or group?

- Describe the person or persons.

- What are people saying to you?

- Where are you?

- Are you outside or inside?

- Describe the countryside to yourself.

- What is the weather like?

- Are you near a body of water?

- Mountains? Pasture? Jungle? Desert?

- In a room of a simple house?

- A castle?

- A cave?

- Describe it. Feel it. See it. Hear it. Let your senses become acute.

- Be patient and let the clarity arise of its own accord.

- If you are unsure, confused, or don't perceive anything, make it up.

Don't be worried that you might be wrong or mistaken. Nothing is erroneous or incorrect in this experience. You are learning to trust yourself and to have faith in whatever is revealed for yourself. Let the answers pop into your head.

- What does this event mean to you?

- If you are unsure or don't know, make it up.

- What are your emotions?

- Did you create any decisions based on this event?

If you find yourself getting upset, take a deep breath, slowly exhale and relax. This method is not meant to bring you pain, rather illumination and release. If you wish, you may detach yourself from any upsetting feelings and simply be an observer.

- Take a long deep breath and slowly exhale. Relax.

After you have thoroughly examined this experience to your satisfaction, go to the next important event of your life.

THE 2ND IMPORTANT EVENT OF THAT LIFE

Go there now.

- How old are you during this event?

- What are the circumstances of this event?

- Use all your senses to experience it. Feel it, see it, hear what is happening.

- Are you with an individual or group?

- What are they saying to you?

- Are there any scents you can discern?

- Can you hear any sounds?

- Where are you?

- Are you outside or inside?

- What is the weather like?

- Describe the countryside.

- Are you near a body of water? Mountains? Pasture? Jungle? Desert?

- Are you in a room of a house? A castle? A cave? A village?

- Describe it for yourself. Feel it. See it. Hear it. Smell it.

- Be patient and let the clarity arise of its own accord.

- If you are unsure, confused, or don't perceive anything, make it up.

Let go of worry that you might be wrong or mistaken. Nothing is erroneous or incorrect in this experience. You are learning to trust yourself and to have faith in whatever comes up for yourself. Answers will simply pop into your head.

What does this 2nd event mean to you? If you are unsure or don't know, *make it up*.

- What emotions do you feel?

- Did you make any decisions based on this event?

If you find yourself getting upset, take a deep breath, slowly exhale and relax. This method is not meant to bring you pain, rather illumination and release. You can float above the situation to feel more detached.

- Is this event connected in any way to the first event?

- Take your time to soak in all the details of this event.

- Take a breath in and exhale. Relax.

- What do these 2 events mean to you? Is this 2nd event connected in any important way to the other event? Do they fit together? In what way? If you are unsure or don't know, make it up.

- Is this event or lifetime connected to people you know today in your current lifetime? Describe. Take your time to soak in all the details of this event.

AFTER YOU HAVE THOROUGHLY EXAMINED THIS EXPERI-ENCE TO YOUR SATISFACTION, GO TO THE MOMENT JUST BEFORE YOUR DEATH IN THAT LIFETIME.

- Be there now.

- How old are you?

- What is your physical condition?

- How did you get to that condition?

- Are one or more people with you?

- Who are they?

- What did they mean to you?

- If no one is there with you, why not?

- Is there anyone with you that you recognize from your current lifetime?

- How did your life change before your death? Was it for the better? Was it for the worse?

- What do you think about that lifetime as you look at these events?

- Are there any emotions? Regrets? Resolutions? Decisions?

- Take a slow, deep breath and let it out. Relax.

- Now relax and let yourself slide out of your physical body as you sense your body dying. Feel release and peace as you do so.

- As you rise towards the sky, imagine a brilliant gold luminescence above you. Waiting there for you is your Higher Self, who is a bright light, filled with love. You feel joy and relief at seeing your Higher Self and the Higher Self is joyful to be with you as well.

- You merge with your Higher Self effortlessly and you feel the delight and ecstasy of that reunion.

- As you do so, you turn your attention towards the body and the life you have just exited. You now have infinite knowledge and wisdom to understand that life. You can receive messages from within your Higher Self. If you get stuck, make it up.

- What did you finish in that life?

- Did you leave anything undone?

- Did you accomplish what you had set out to do?

- Did you meet the souls you intended to meet?

- Is there any grief remaining in the body and life you have just departed? Remorse? Bitterness? Anger? Sadness?

- What other emotions did you have upon dying?

- Did you make any decisions as what you want to do in the future for further learning, growth and evolution and to balance the scales of that life?

- Do you recognize any of the people you knew in that life as being in your current life?

- If so, who are they in your present lifetime?

- What is the type and quality of your relationship with each person that you knew while in that other lifetime?

- **As you assimilate all this information, take a breath and liberate the knowledge. Breathe out all your emotions and decisions and let them depart. Watch them rise like weightless hot air balloons up into the gold light above you where they dissolve easily and gently, evaporating into nothingness.**

- Thank yourself for receiving the knowledge of the lifetime you have just observed.

- Allow forgiveness and gratitude for who you were and what you learned to flood into your awareness.

- Thank all the people who participated in that life with you, no matter how easy or difficult each relationship had been.

- Take a deep breath and slowly exhale. Relax.

NOW WE WILL MOVE ON TO EXPLORE LEMURIA...

Exit through the door you entered from that prior life, get back into your boat, release it from its mooring, and begin once again to travel back along the River of Time.

When you find the mooring on the River of Time that leads to your life in Lemuria, guide your boat there. Fasten your boat at the dock, get out, and walk up the pier to your destination.

At the end of the pier is a closed door. Open the door and walk in, closing it behind you. Now you will repeat the steps you took in the first lifetime you examined.

- In front of you is a mirror. Look into it and examine the person you see there. That person is you in that Lemurian lifetime.

- Are you male or female?

- Old or young?

- What color is your hair?

- Your eyes?

- How are you dressed?

- Next to the mirror is a calendar. What is the year? If you are un-decided, make it up. A date will pop into your mind. It most likely will be thousands of years ago. Make it up.

- Ask yourself "what is my age?" If you don't know or can't decide, make it up. An age will pop into your mind which might be hun-dreds or even thousands of years old.

GO TO THE FIRST IMPORTANT EVENT OF THAT LEMURIAN LIFE.

- How old are you during this event?

- What are the circumstances of this event?

- Use all your senses to experience it. Feel it, see it, hear what is happening.

- What are people saying to you?

- Are there any scents you can discern?

- Can you hear any sounds?

- Where are you? Are you outside or inside? What is the weather like?

- Describe the countryside.

- Are you near a body of water? Mountains? Pasture? Jungle? Desert?

- Are you in a room of a house? A cave?

- Describe it to yourself. See it. Touch it.

- Are you with an individual or a group? *Be patient and let the clarity arise of its own accord. If you are unsure, confused, or don't perceive anything, make it up. Don't be worried that you might be wrong or mistaken. Nothing is erroneous or incorrect in this experience. You are learning to trust yourself and to have faith in whatever comes up for yourself.*

- What does this event mean to you? If you are unsure or don't know, make it up.

- What are your emotions? What are you feeling?

- Did you create any decisions based on this event?

If you find yourself getting upset, take a deep breath, exhale slowly and relax. This method is not meant to bring you pain, rather illumination and release. If you wish, you may detach yourself from any upsetting feelings and be an observer. Take another long deep breath and slowly exhale.

AFTER YOU HAVE THOROUGHLY INVESTIGATED THAT EVENT TO YOUR SATISFACTION, GO TO THE NEXT IMPORTANT (2ND) EVENT OF YOUR LEMURIAN LIFETIME.

Go there now.

How old are you during this event? What are the circumstances of this event?

- Use all your senses to experience it. Feel it, see it, hear what is happening.

- Are there people with you? Describe the individual or group.

- What are they saying to you?

- Are there any scents you can discern?

- Can you hear any sounds?

- Where are you? Are you outside or inside? What is the weather like? Describe the countryside to yourself.

- Are you near a body of water? Mountains? Pasture? In a room of a house? A cave?

Describe it. Touch it. See it. Hear it. Smell it.

Be patient and let the clarity arise of its own accord. If you are unsure, confused, or don't perceive anything, make it up. Don't be worried that you could be wrong or mistaken. Nothing is erroneous or incorrect in this experience.

- You are learning to trust yourself and to have faith in whatever comes up for yourself.

- What does this event mean to you? If you are unsure or don't know, make it up.

- What are your emotions?

- If you find yourself getting upset, take a deep breath, exhale slowly and relax. This method is not meant to bring you pain, rather illumination and release. You can float above the situation to feel more detached.

- What does this second event mean to you? If you are unsure or don't know, make it up.

- Did you make any decisions based on this event?

- Is this event connected in any way to the first event?

- Take your time to soak in all the details of this event.

- Take a breath in and exhale. Relax.

AFTER YOU HAVE THOROUGHLY INVESTIGATED THIS SECOND EXPERIENCE TO YOUR SATISFACTION, GO TO THE NEXT IMPORTANT (3RD) EVENT OF YOUR LEMURIAN LIFETIME.

- Go there now.

- How old are you during this event? What are the circumstances of this event?

- Use all your senses to experience it. Feel it, see it, hear what is happening.

- Are there any scents you can discern?

- Can you hear any sounds?

- Where are you? Are you outside or inside? What is the weather like?

- Describe the countryside to yourself. Are you near a body of water? Mountains? Pasture? In a room of a house? A cave?

- Describe it to yourself. Feel it. See it. Hear it.

- Are you with an individual or group?

- What are people saying to you?

- What is the action you observe? Are you part of it?
  Be patient and let the clarity arise of its own accord.

If you are unsure, confused, or don't perceive anything, make it up. Don't be worried that you could be wrong or mistaken. Nothing is erroneous or incorrect in this experience. You are learning to trust yourself and to have faith in whatever comes up for yourself.

- What does this event mean to you? If you are unsure or don't know, make it up.

- What are your emotions?

- Did you create any decisions based on this event?

- If you find yourself getting upset, take a deep breath, exhale slowly and relax. This method is not meant to bring you pain, rather illumination and release. You can float above the situation to feel more detached.

What do these 3 events mean to you? How do they fit together?

- If you are unsure or don't know, *make it up.* You can jot down notes in your notebook to remember.

- What are your emotions?

- Is this event connected in any way to the first or second events?

- Take your time to soak in all the details of this event.

- What does this third event mean to you? If you are unsure or don't know, make it up.

- Did you make any decisions based on all 3 events?

- Is this event connected to any persons you know in your current lifetime?

Take your time to soak in all the details of this event.

AFTER YOU HAVE THOROUGHLY INVESTIGATED THE 3RD EXPERIENCE TO YOUR SATISFACTION, TAKE A BREATH, LET IT OUT AND RELAX. NOW YOU WILL MOVE TO THE MOMENT JUST BEFORE DEATH IN YOUR LEMURIAN LIFETIME.

- How old are you? What is your physical condition?

- How did you get to that condition?

- Are one or more people with you? Who are they? What did they mean to you? Are they people you know today in your current lifetime? If no one is there, why not?

- How did your life change before your death? For the better? For the worse?

- What do you think about your Lemurian lifetime as you look at these events?

- Do you have any emotions? Regrets? Resolutions? Did you make any decisions as you are dying?

Take a slow, deep breath and exhale.

- Now relax and let yourself slide out of your physical body as you sense your body dying. Feel the release and peace as you do so.

- As you rise towards the sky, imagine a brilliant gold light above you. Waiting there for you is your Higher Self who is a bright light, filled with love. You feel joy and relief at seeing your Higher Self and the Higher Self is happy in seeing you as well.

- You merge into that Self effortlessly and you feel the delight and ecstasy of that reintegration.

- As you do so, you turn your attention towards the Lemurian body and the life you have just exited. You now have infinite knowledge and wisdom to understand that life. You can receive messages from within your Higher Self.

- What did you finish in that life?

- Did you leave anything undone?

- Did you accomplish what you had set out to do?

- Did you meet the souls you intended to meet?

- Is there any grief remaining in that body and the life you have just left? Remorse? Bitterness? Anger? Sadness?

- What other emotions did you have upon dying?

- Did you make any decisions as what you want to do in the future for further learning, growth and evolution and to balance the scales of that life?

- Do you recognize any of the people you knew in that life as being in your current life? If so, who are they in your present lifetime? What is the quality of your relationship with each person that you knew while there?

As you assimilate all this information, take a deep breath and exhale, liberating the knowledge. Let go of all your emotions and decisions. Watch those rise into the gold light above you and dissolve easily and gently, evaporating into light.

- Thank yourself for receiving the knowledge of this lifetime you have observed and allow forgiveness and gratitude for who you were flood into your awareness.

- Thank each person who participated in that life with you, no matter how easy or difficult each relationship had been.

- Take a deep breath and slowly exhale. Relax.

Now it is time to return home.

Exit through the door you entered, get back into the boat, release it from its mooring, and return home along the River of Time.

When you return, get out of the boat. You're back in present time.

- Take a deep breath and slowly exhale. Stretch your arms. Feel your feet on the ground. Feel the chair beneath you.

- Open your eyes and look around. Pick up your logical mind and put it back in place.

- Realize that you have taken an extraordinary journey in search of yourself.

- The lifetimes and events you uncovered and experienced will help in therapeutic changes to your current self, relationships, health, finances, and attitude.

- You can return to this method again and again, to learn, recover, heal, and awaken more fully into the pleasure and knowledge of who you are in this lifetime. Congratulations!

***

RITUAL GROUP MEDITATION TRAVELING IN YOUR ETHERIC BODY TO MT. SHASTA — EXERCISE #4

This is the time you can practice attending the ritual group meditation as you did at the end of Class #1. Although you may want to skip this exercise, I encourage you to repeat it often as it will potentiate your growth.

Tape recorder or cellphone: You can use a tape recorder or a cellphone to make a recording of the original exercise to or go to YouTube "Mt Shasta meditation exercise #4."

Notebook: Journal your experiences when finished.

***

Traveling on the River of Time, Lauren O. Thyme © 2017
The Nine Waves of Creation, Dr. Carl Calleman, © 2016

LIVING IN THE NEW LEMURIA:

EXERCISES, PRACTICES, AND TECHNIQUES

Class #4
Discernment

Lauren's Law #24: "Pay attention as if your life depends on it. It does."

Developing one's own discernment takes time while "paying attention" to messages, events and experiences, and then following where they lead you. Discernment works through feeling in the body. Without feeling it is only knowledge and information without earthly connection.

You have "Divine Software" built into your consciousness, DNA and the very fiber of your being, that allows for connection and communication to and from the Divine – what I call Creator Source Operating System, or CSOS. You and Creator Source are absolutely compatible. You can download support, love, compassion, peace and unity from Creator Source. I go one step further and contend that Creator Source wants what you want, and you want what Creator Source wants.

***

LEMURIAN STAR – MERKABA – SACRED GEOMETRY
EXERCISE #7

Activity: You have purchased gold or yellow yarn – enough to make an out-line of a 6-pointed star on your floor that is large enough for you to sit inside. This will be a replica of a Lemurian star.

Using the yarn make an outline of a 6-pointed star on your floor large enough to sit within. Although you may think this activity is silly, the energy to which the Star is connected is immense and linked to other sacred geometry includ-ing pyramids, tetrahedrons and the Merkaba.

The word Merkaba is composed of three separate words: Mer, which means light, Ka, which means spirit and Ba, which means Body. Put together, these three words connote the union of spirit with the body, surrounded by light. The symbol, which takes the shape of a star, is believed to be a divine vehicle made entirely of light and designed to transport or connect the spirit and body to higher realms. Ancient Jewish texts reveal that the word is also the Hebrew word for a divine chariot.

The easiest way to do this is to lay out one triangle, fasten it, then lay a second triangle over it. Practice creating this Star to do meditations and exercises within. You will do exercises sitting inside your Gold Star. If you find you cannot comfortably sit on the floor within the Star, then bring a chair into the center. If you wish you can add crystals to the center of the Star making sure you have room for yourself and a chair if necessary.

Part of what you are learning is to pay close attention to energy and energy shifts. In a later class, I will discuss how to Feng Shui your home. Doing Feng

Shui stimulates and makes energy flow and expand throughout various areas of your life.

Please seat yourself within the Lemurian Star. Feel the energy inside.

Notice what the energy feels like when you set it up.

Notebook: Write down your experience. What does the Lemurian Star energy feel like? What do you notice? You are learning how to shift energy at will.

***

GIVING AND RECEIVING – THE UNIVERSAL BANK ACCOUNT

Unity in the form of the Lemurian Way and the 9th wave requires a flow back and forth between Creator Source and individuals, groups, nations and the world. "Being Nice" by giving or graciously receiving is more than good manners. It is necessary to learn to flow and increase spiritually relevant energy by giving and receiving. The same idea is true with giving and receiving to and from Creator Source. Since 2011 Planet Earth is in a learning curve of co-creation in which we are becoming partners with the Universe.

Because "everything is connected to everything," giving and receiving are fused in a seamless flow of energy that I call the Universal Bank Account. It's the natural movement of the Universe. Here is a simple diagram of how the Universal Bank Account works.

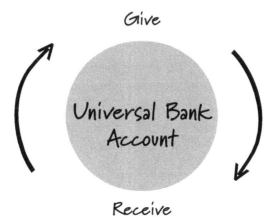

The Universal Bank Account is not just about money. The Universe contains an explicit connection between giving and receiving. The connection is like a revolving door, similar to Sir Isaac Newton's law of motion: "For every action there is an equal and opposite reaction." When a person gives, the Universe is then obligated to give back, to return energy to the sender, or else the Universe would become unbalanced. The person receives from the Universe. It only appears that a person receives from someone or something else. In truth, however, it is the Universe giving back through whatever means it has at its disposal. The most wonderful part of this dual motion is that the energy that is sent to you may not show up immediately. That energy goes into your Universal Bank Account. When you need something at a future date like money, a job, help fixing a tire, friendliness or a hug, the Universe supplies it, withdrawing energy from your Universal Bank Account. Energy moves in an endless loop, a cycle, through giving, then receiving, giving and receiving into infinity.

Is this spiritual? Several of my friends have questioned my theory, asking whether it was spiritual or not. They're worried about manipulating the Universe. I tell them that Giving and Receiving is the active Universe. We can simply notice and play its wonderful pastime. Thus, it is intrinsically spiritual. When people tithe at church, they expect it to be multiplied back to them, often at more than the 10% they donated to the collection plate.

GIVING AND RECEIVING — EXERCISE #9

Every day give **at least** one "something" – **without being asked** . . A smile. A sincere compliment. A helping hand. Your place in line at the grocery store. Allowing the car ahead of you to pull ahead. Putting out wild bird seed. Giving away clothes to someone who needs clothes or items to a thrift store. Giving money to a worthwhile cause. Pulling weeds in a disabled neighbor's yard. Calling a friend. Look around to see what might be needed. Giving adds not only to your Universal Bank Account, but also to the Universal Bank Account for Earth as well.

GIVING: Practice giving at least once a day, more if you can – on purpose and consciously. Every time you give, stay aware and conscious that you are stimulating the Universal Bank Account of abundance for yourself and others.

RECEIVING: When someone compliments *you* or gives *you* something, simply reply "Thank you." More is unnecessary. **Keep it simple.** Stay **aware** and **conscious** that you are stimulating the Universal Bank Account for yourself and others by receiving on purpose and consciously.

Practice both giving and receiving daily.

With practice you will discover that after a while you won't know if you are giving or receiving at any given time. Receiving will begin to feel like giving – and giving will feel like receiving. It seems magical because the Universe originally set up the circular flow and it happens effortlessly.

Lauren's Law #24: "Pay attention as if your life depends on it. It does."

Lauren's Law #12: "When you need something, give."

Lauren's Law #3: "If it's easy, it's right."

If you're not receiving, check to make sure you are practicing giving on a daily basis.

If you're still not receiving, check to make sure you are open to receiving. The rest is divine timing.

Lauren's Law #13: "The universe is all about timing. So is everything in your life."

All day - every day - pay close attention, as if your life depends on it. It does.

Thank Creator Source for every miracle, large and small. For smiles. For people. For good fortune, even if something arrives that you were expecting.

***

GRATITUDE LIST EXERCISE #10

Notebook:

Take out your notebook and turn to a new page.

Write today's date at the top of the page.

Underneath write the words "I am grateful for…."

Now **list** at least 5 things you are grateful for. Big, little, complex, simple.

Simply write them down.

Do this every day. List at least 5 things you are grateful for.

You may even want to buy a special Gratitude Notebook to do this practice.

Being grateful is essential, as problems, challenges, disappointments, ill health, loss, unhappy people, situations, and feelings arise to draw our attention away from perfection.

Lauren's Law #11: "When a difficult situation arrives in your life, love that situation, forgive and be grateful. The Universe has sent that situation to you as a gift for your learning."

Be sure to include at least one item that seems **difficult** to be grateful for – like a flat tire, bouncing a check, forgetting an appointment, or catching a cold. This is an extremely potent form of gratitude which shifts your consciousness.

Now **write down** at least 1 thing you are grateful for that seems difficult.

Practice both forms of gratitude – easy and difficult – every day.

Notebook: Write about your experiences of this exercise.

***

CREATOR SOURCE CONTAINER — EXERCISE #11

Get out your Creator Source Container. Pick up a slip of paper.

What do you need or want today? Big, little, complex, simple?

Write that need or want on one of the slips.

Place the slip in your Creator Source Container, pausing a moment with your hand over the top. Visualize gold light streaming down from Creator Source into the container, then thank Creator Source for granting you that desire. Visualize and feel that it is already accomplished. This is similar to what you learned in chapter #2.

Let's try another one. What else do you need or want today? Pick up another slip of paper. Write what you desire on it.

Place the slip in your Creator Source Container, pausing a moment with your hand over the top. Visualize gold light streaming down from Creator Source, then thank Creator Source for granting you that desire. Visualize and feel that it is already accomplished.

You can ask Creator Source to help you with something intangible that you wish for, like healing a health issue or wanting to remove a difficulty with an individual. What do you want fixed, "healed," removed or ameliorated today?

Pick up a slip of paper. Write that intangible desire on it.

Place the slip in your Creator Source Container, pausing a moment with your hand over the top. Visualize gold light streaming down from Creator Source into the container, then thank Creator Source for granting you that desire. Visualize and feel that it is already accomplished.

Store your Creator Source Container in a Sacred Place - like your altar - where you will see it regularly. You can surround it with crystals or other sacred objects. You'll continue working with the Creator Source Container in later chapters.

Notebook: Write about your experience of this exercise.

***

HOW TO EASILY GET WHAT YOU WANT — EXERCISE #12
by writing a Creator Source letter

excerpt from *Cosmic Grandma Wisdom* © 2017

I'm not just suggesting that you can get what you want. I'm telling you emphatically!! I have used this method for over forty years, and it works fabulously. Whenever I want something new, I write a new Creator Source Letter. I usually get 85% of the specifics, sometimes more than 100% because of bonuses.

A person doesn't need to believe in a higher power. A person can be an agnostic or atheist and this method will still work great for them. You can call it the "Universe" letter if you want. One thing we can all agree on is that we live in the universe. I call it the Creator Source Letter for simplicity.

The "Creator Source Letter" consists of a few simple steps. Mostly, the letter is a brainstorming device, which signals your request to the "Field of all Possibilities," as Deepak Chopra calls the un-manifested universe. You're going to be manifesting something out of nothing, a little bit like your own personal Big Bang.

Now, get out a large piece of paper and a pen or pencil. Be sure to make your writing legible, neat, and tidy. You want the Universe to clearly know what you are asking to manifest.

1 – Write down **the current date (day/month/year)** at the top.

2 – write **Dear Creator Source:**

3 – write **I.......** (write your full name here) **NOW HAVE the PERFECT........**

This could be a job, car, house, apartment, housekeeper, employee, employer, career, vacation, total healing from a physical problem - whatever you desire. Limit this letter to just one manifestation. You can always write more letters.

Write it down.

I want means that you are lacking… Replace that with **"I now have"**

The word "NOW" is potent. Just ask Eckhardt Tolle. Manifestation exists in the NOW.

"Perfect" implies what you strongly desire with many desired attributes.

I suggest you start with a simple request. This helps you become acquainted with how to do the process and to build your manifestation muscles. Not to mention it will give your skeptical mind something stress-free to work on and work up to. You may want to write a series of letters. You can then clearly see what you're willing to allow into your life by what shows up! With practice you will be able to manifest better and with greater ease. That has been my experience.

4 – Details: (here is where you're going to put your brain, heart, and imagination to work)

Take a few minutes to brainstorm.

Notebook: List every single feature you can think of that would describe your perfect... (Fill in the blank).

Make this list as detailed as possible. Leave nothing out, no matter how far-fetched it seems to you. Forget your logical mind while doing your list. Your list does **NOT** have to make sense. Your list does NOT have to be "practical." Put fear on the backburner and stand courageous.

Don't assume anything. The Universe is not a mind-reader. You have to ask for what you desire. Creator Source wants us to have what we desire. Be specific. Write it down.

Include a TARGET DATE — month/day/year. This helps the Universe know when you expect your manifestation. Make your date reasonable. You'll know what that means.

Write this entire detailed list in your letter.

5 — After you've finished your detailed list, write these exact words: *"This or something better now manifests for the good of all concerned."*

The reason for this sentence is:

— You don't want to limit yourself to what you have asked for. The Universe may want to give you more!

— "For the good of all concerned" You don't want to take something away from someone else. This phrase protects your integrity. Your request benefits others in ways you may not see at this time.

— You want this manifestation to be for your own highest good as well as that for others.

6 — Then write, "Thank you, Creator Source."

Gratitude is a powerful spiritual vibration, bringing good things your way, as did the Gratitude list earlier.

7 — Sign your name the way you wrote it at the top of the letter.

8 — Post this letter somewhere where you can see it every day, like on the bathroom mirror or refrigerator. Although you have included a target date, you may receive your manifestation sooner — or later — than you have written. The Universe operates with synchronicities, so it must arrange and orchestrate your manifestation. Relax. The Creator Source Letter is a process.

Notebook: Write about your experience of this exercise.

***

Gregg Braden, in his book *Resilience of the Heart,* writes: "When we choose to feel feelings such as appreciation, gratitude, forgiveness, care and compassion [pieces of Gold Light Wisdom] that creates what is called coherence in our bodies. Science is now documenting that when we feel those feelings, they are mirrored in the field and everyone benefits from the experience of the relative few. It is documented that if we can create this effect with a certain number of people [equaling] the **square root of one percent of a given population** [known as the Maharishi Effect], then we will have this outcome."
The Hundredth Monkey Theory[1] explains that the more of us working to shift the planet, the faster it will develop. In order for the shift to happen, a critical mass, the Maharishi effect, must be achieved.

***

Remember the word chant exercise mantra from Class 1 that reviews Gold Light Wisdom? It's worth repeating. You may say aloud, pausing after each word or phrase:

I now have:
- —Unconditional love of self and others…
- —Acceptance and allowing…
- —Blamelessness…
- —Willingness…
- —Noticing without criticism…
- —Forgiveness of self and others…
- —Patience…
- —Mutual respect…
- —Mutual support…
- —Detachment…
- —Living in present time…
- —Open and loving communication…
- —Trust in and surrender to a higher power…
- —Gratitude…
- —Defenselessness and neutrality…
- —Giving and receiving…
- —Joyful creation…
- —Feeling my emotions…
- —Empathy and compassion…
- —Psychic abilities and telepathy…
- —Having fun…
- —Doing what I love…
- —Loving what I do…
- —Unity…
- —Harmony…
- —Peace…
- —Thank you, Creator Source!!

Excerpt from *The Lemurian Way* © 1994

***

RITUAL GROUP MEDITATION EXERCISE TRAVELING IN YOUR ETHERIC BODY TO MT. SHASTA – EXERCISE #4

This is the time you can practice attending the ritual group meditation as you did at the end of Class #1. Although you may want to skip this exercise, I encourage you to repeat it often as it will stimulate your growth.

Tape recorder or cellphone: You can use a tape recorder or a cellphone to make a recording of the original exercise to or go to YouTube to listen to the descriptions.

Notebook: Journal your experiences when finished.

***

If you have questions or concerns, you may send me an email at *thyme.lauren@gmail.com.*

***

At this point you may "take down" – remove - your Lemurian 6-pointed star formation. As you do so, pay attention to discerning an energy shift. Can you feel the difference?

Notebook: Write down experiences, insights and transformations you had in Class #4. Write down your experiences with the Lemurian Star.

***

[1]*The Hundredth Monkey*, Ken Keyes, Jr. © 1984
The Nine Waves of Creation, Dr. Carl Calleman © 2016
Cosmic Grandma Wisdom, Lauren O. Thyme © 2017
The Lemurian Way, Remembering Your Essential Nature, Lauren O. Thyme © 2000

LIVING IN THE NEW LEMURIA:

EXERCISES, PRACTICES, AND TECHNIQUES

Class #5
Thoughts and Emotions

***

LEMURIAN STAR – MERKABA – SACRED GEOMETRY

Before you begin the next group of exercises in this class, set up your Star. Did you feel the energy change or shift when you set it up?

Please seat yourself within the gold star. Imagine Gold Light streaming into the Lemurian star. Feel the energy inside. Part of what you are learning as an Elder-in-training is to pay close attention to energy and energy shifts and learn to shift energy at will. Using the 6-pointed Lemurian Star will help you increase and change energy.

Contemplate: What does this energy feel like?

Notebook: Write down your observations.

***

LAUREN'S LAW #5: M = ET²

This translates to Miracles/Matter/Manifestation/Time .... Equals .... Energized (spiritual) Thought Squared .... (of **Two** or more people).

Miracles of physical matter, events, space, or time can be sped up, increased or transformed through the energized, spiritual interaction of two or more people. One person plus one person equals **more** than two people. Two people plus two people equals **MUCH** more than four people. The increase of energy is exponential. This is one of the principles of the Lemurian Way which is one reason why Lemurians worked in groups. Also, you are part of the 9th wave of creation from the Mayan Calendar which is about unity and conscious co-creation.

Therefore, you might want to invite your friends to join you in this work as each of you will gain more than working alone. The learning, growth and evolution of those who practice Living in the New Lemuria grows on an exponential curve because of the action of $M = ET^2$

***

VOICE FIGHTING EXERCISE — #13

Lauren's Law #27: "The mind is not my friend."

Now it is time to focus on unpleasant, difficult and upsetting emotions along with different methods of working with them and reducing or even omitting their impact.

Below are some exercises which strengthen **awareness**, an important piece of Gold Light Wisdom. Class #5 is geared to shine a spotlight on uncomfortable emotions which interfere with one's life and happiness as well block spiritual interactions, and dilute the power of $M = ET^2$

Thoughts lead to emotions. We all have disharmonious thoughts and emotions that arise sometimes. Rather than fighting yourself, blaming yourself, or feeling that thoughts and emotions are a hopeless battle, I have an exercise for you.

Do you have emotions that recur throughout your day? Repeat throughout your life? There are 6 major emotions that the NEGATIVE VOICE inside you amuses itself with, what Buddhists call the Monkey Mind.

Voice fighting is the name of your first practice. You will be learning to notice without judgment: using acceptance, surrender, defenselessness, and neutrality of both thoughts and emotions. Mindfulness is noticing which emotions are active while being non-judgmental of those emotions.

Notebook: get out your notebook and turn to a new page.
Make 2 columns.

At the top of 1ˢᵗ column, write THOUGHT.

At the top of the secod column, write EMOTION.

Homework: Keep a record for a week to simply **notice** thoughts — and whether disharmonious emotions arise after those thoughts.

During the week plan to spend a few minutes every day noticing an emotion. Put that in the second column.

Next notice a thought that arose just before the emotion. Put that in the first column.

Notice trends. Do you have any thoughts or emotions that recur at intervals? Do you notice a reappearance of specific thoughts? A return of a particular emotion? Do you notice some thoughts and emotions occur more frequently than others? Does anything stimulate those thoughts and emotions to occur?

Do you notice a downward shift of energy or mood? Chances are the VOICE is responsible, talking loudly in your ear, insistently demanding your attention.

Here are the six favorite destructive emotion games the VOICE likes to play:

    Depression
    Anxiety
    Guilt
    Irrational fear
    Hopelessness
    Helplessness

We'll return to Voice Fighting in Class #6 to continue to learn how to re-train your mind (thoughts). In the meantime, simply notice and write down what you observe without judgment.

Doing the Voice Fighting work helps with emotional release as those Voice emotions are persistent and negative, also known as habitual patterns. These patterns can be from this lifetime, other lifetimes, and also through genetic DNA and your family.

Lauren's Law #24: "Pay attention as if your life depends on it. It does."

If a person doesn't release emotions, those go into their body, causing problems, ultimately to create physical dysfunction, disease, and even death. I encourage you to be proactive in dealing with disturbing emotions because they can damage you, your life and relationships if ignored.

A major study by Kaiser Permanente reported "…that considerable and prolonged emotional stress in childhood has life-long consequences for a person's health and well-being…such stress can lead to serious problems such as alcoholism, depression, eating disorders, unsafe sex, HIV/AIDS, heart disease, cancer, and other chronic diseases."

Notebook: Write down your experiences and any thoughts you have about Voice Fighting.

***

THE JOHN TRAVOLTA EMOTION SURRENDER DANCE — EXERCISE #14

You are invited to practice what Lauren calls the *John Travolta Emotional Surrender Dance* (from his famous disco scene in the movie Saturday Night Fever). You learned this dance in Class #1.

First, think of a disturbing emotion or feel one you already have.

Imagine Creator Source to your **Right** and above you. Offer the emotion with your *right* hand to Creator Source and say, "Here, God" or "Here, Goddess" or "Here, Universe" or whatever name you choose to call it. Imagine that Creator Source has now taken the emotion off your hands.

Next, imagine Creator Source to your **Left** and above you. Offer the unwanted emotion with your **left** hand to Creator Source and say, "Here, God" "Here, Goddess" "Here, Universe" or whatever name you choose to call it. Imagine that Creator Source has now taken the emotion off your hands again.

Finally, imagine you have released the emotion to Creator Source by saying the words I'm "staying alive." **

***

SURRENDER UNWANTED EMOTIONS TO YOUR CREATOR SOURCE CONTAINER — EXERCISE #15

Activity: Have your Creator Source Container near you. Have your slips of paper ready and a pen.

Steps:

Get comfortable. Take a deep breath and slowly exhale. As you do, become more relaxed.

Next, imagine that Creator Source is floating above you in a giant warm bubble of gold light like the sun. Gold Light was used by the Lemurians for all their sacred rituals and is the most powerful light in the Universe for transformation. Whatever your chosen name is, focus on Creator Source right now.

Ask Creator Source to send Gold Light Blessings into your body through the top of your head. Feel the gold light warmth and peaceful flow as it enters your body. Allow it to radiate throughout your head, into your body, arms, legs and feet, then into the ground below you…

Deeply breathe again and feel the blessings you are receiving from Creator Source. You feel ever more relaxed and receptive.

When you are ready, think of a disturbing emotion you have had recently or are having right now. Write the disturbing emotion on a slip of paper and place it lovingly in the Creator Source Container.

When you have placed the emotion in the Creator Source Container, put your hand over the top of the container and ask Creator Source to bless the emotion and yourself with Gold Light. Ask Creator Source aloud for this blessing. Do this now…

Feel the blessing emanating to you. You may see Gold Light fill up your Container. You may smell flowers or fragrances arising from the blessing. You may intuitively taste a special food that you enjoy. You may hear lovely music. Take your time in this process. Linger in the glow of the blessings you receive. You may experience delight that you can enjoy Creator Source's blessing…

Now remove your hand from the Container and let go of the emotion, knowing that you have been blessed by an infinitely loving Source…

Now you will go into an even deeper level practicing unity, harmony, and blessings in an entirely new way – using willingness and acceptance, both highly elevated states of spiritual being.

Take a deep breath and focus on the Gold Light still streaming into your head and body from Creator Source…

Say the following words aloud, "I accept this emotion. I am willing to release this emotion." Willingness and acceptance are illuminating spiritual parts of wisdom with great power to heal both yourself and the planet. Feel acceptance and willingness enter your body from Creator Source, filling you with a blissful, peaceful knowing, as the Golden Light imbues you…

Take another deep breath, gently exhale and relax. You can say aloud, "*Everything is perfect, no matter what it looks like, for the purpose of learning, growth and evolution.*"

HIGHER SELF EMOTIONAL RELEASE — EXERCISE #16

The purpose of this exercise is to release disharmonious feelings and emotions and to discover the reasons you are feeling them. You can do this exercise even if you are feeling someone else's feelings and emotions otherwise known as Empathic. It can also work for those Conduits among us who are currently feeling the emotional overload from their 144,000 people. We will discuss Empaths and Conduits in Class #11.

Record: You can record these instructions on a tape recorder or cellphone.

Alternative idea: You can ask someone to read these instructions to you and help you with the following dialogues

1. Close your eyes. Take a deep breath. Relax...

2. Remove your logical mind. Set it aside...

3. "What am I feeling?" Identify and speak aloud disharmonious or uncomfortable feeling(s)...

4. Float upwards and connect with your Higher Self...

5. Ask Higher Self, "why am I feeling disharmonious feeling(s)?

6. Higher Self answers aloud in explanation. "You are feeling ... because...."

7. Say aloud to Higher Self, "Please release this feeling(s)" It will feel like bubbles rising to the surface of a pond.

    [If you are not feeling a release of feelings, do not continue. Here are further steps you can take]

7a. Float down and ask lower self: "Where in my body am I feeling disharmonious feelings?" Point to place(s) with finger.

7b. Ask the first place in your body, "What do you want to tell me?"

7c. Body responds until complete. (You may start to feel release here)

7d. Ask second place in your body, "What do you want to tell me?"

7e. Body responds until complete. (You may start to feel release here)

7f.. Ask any other place in your body: "What do you want to tell me?"

7g. Body responds. (You may start to feel release here)

7h. You, "Thank you, body." Float back to Higher Self. "Higher Self, is there anything else you want to tell me?"

7i. Higher Self responds "yes, there is" or "no, there is not." If yes, Higher Self continues to explain. If no, go to 8 below.

7j. "Yes" Higher Self speaks and explains. (You may start to feel strong release here)

7k. Say aloud to Higher Self, "Please release feeling(s)" It will feel like bubbles rising to the surface of a pond.

8. Feel the bubbles of disharmonious feeling float away until gone. If not, return to dialoguing with body and Higher Self until you feel a release, a shift of energy and consciousness while the feeling(s) dissipate.

9. If you're doing this on your own, feel the bubbles rise... If another person is directing this exercise, that person may also feel the bubbles rise as the disharmonious feeling(s) dissipates until gone.

10. "Thank you, Higher Self…" Breathe and relax. Return to your lower self. Put your logical mind back in place. Open your eyes. Thank yourself.

Notebook: Write down your experience.

***

RISING ABOVE EMOTIONS

In addition to surrendering emotions using the exercises above, one can also "go up the scale of emotions" to a more desirable emotion.

We all have mirror neurons inside the frontal cortex of our brain. A **mirror neuron is a** type of sensory-motor cell located in the brain that is activated when an individual performs an action or observes another individual performing the same action. Thus, the neurons "mirror" the actions of others. Social behaviorists are studying mirror neurons regarding social behaviors. Dr. Iocoboni, a specialist studying mirror neurons, speculates, "It would be fascinating to see if we can use brain stimulation to change complex moral decisions through impacting the amount of concern people experience for others' pain. It could provide a new method for increasing concern for others' well-being." Could this be another way of saying, "as I transform myself, other people transform themselves in my presence?"

Lauren's Law #26: As I transform myself, other people transform themselves in my presence.

You may find that you may have been reluctant to do work on releasing emotions. You may discover that an emotion falling lower on the chart may feel like a tick that has landed in your emotional field and is resistant to being removed. Emotions in the lower range seem to want to hang on and perpetuate themselves. Yet you will find—with practice—an emotion releases as you move up the chart. As one moves higher, it gets easier to move up. The emotions no longer have that persistent, "I don't want to let go" aspect.

The next practice is based on a chart **Your Instrument Panel** by Lola Jones from her book *Everything Is Going Great in My Absence.* You may want to print out the chart below and keep it handy to repeat this exercise whenever you desire.

I highly recommend doing this exercise with another person, each taking turns to read the entire list of directions to the other, pausing as directed in the script.

Lauren's Law #5: "M = ET²"

Lauren's Law #3: "If it's easy, it's right."

Your Instrument Panel

(as you go up the steps, the more empowered and happier you feel)

Ecstasy *YOU FEEL POWERFUL UP HERE*

Joy, Bliss *You are your Large Self up here.*

Direct Knowing, Empowerment This *energy is light, fast, flowing, un-resisted*

Freedom

Love, Appreciation

Passion, Eagerness, Enthusiasm

Happiness, Positive Expectation
More Expansive Energy, Belief

Optimism, Confidence *I Can Do It*

Hopefulness, Seeing Possibilities, Curiosity

Self Esteem, Interest, Courage

Contentment, Relaxation, Emptiness

Acceptance, Boredom, I Don't Care ————- *The resting zone, not exciting, but useful*

Pessimism, I Give Up —— *THE TIPPING POINT* ————

Frustration, Aggravation, Impatience

Overwhelm, Stressed, Overwork *Much of society lives here and thinks it's normal.*

Disappointment

Doubt, Confusion, Uncertainty

Worry, Negative expectation

Discouragement, I Cannot Do It, Fatigue

Anger *A bridge to get your power/energy back*

Revenge Hatred, Rage *More Contracted Energy*

Jealousy, Desire That Feels Bad, Lack

Guilt, Blame, Projecting Negativity On Others

Fear *You feel powerless down here*

Sadness *The energy is slow, heavy, dense, resistant*

Grief, Depression *It's hard to hear your Large Self down here*

Shame, Unworthiness, Despair

reprinted by permission from Lola Jones, *Things Are Going Great in My Absence*

***

RISING ABOVE EMOTIONS — EXERCISE #17

Steps:

1. Relax in your chair.

2. Look at the chart Your Instrument Panel. Notice without judgment and feel what emotion or group of emotions you are currently feeling and where on the chart that emotion resides.

3. Next notice which emotion or group of emotions is just above the one(s) you currently feel… Say that emotion or group of emotions aloud.

4. Close your eyes. Focusing on the third eye chakra in the middle of your forehead, imagine you can look up through the inside of your head towards the top of your head. Imagine you are taking yourself up an elevator to that next emotion or group of emotions on the chart…

5. Feel what this second emotion or group of emotions feels like in your third eye. Say the emotion's name aloud again... Feel that emotion gain strength inside your third eye. Feel the shift as you do so. Feel any sensations as you feel the shift, especially in your third eye or on the top of your head...

6. When you are ready to up one more step, look at the chart. Notice what emotion or group of emotions you are currently feeling and where on the chart it resides. Now notice which emotion or group of emotions is just above that one and say the name aloud...

7. Close your eyes. Focusing on the third eye chakra in the middle of your forehead, imagine you can look up through the inside of your head towards the top of your head. Imagine you are taking yourself up an elevator to the next higher emotion on the chart...

8. Feel what that emotion or group of emotions feels like in your third eye. Say the emotion's name aloud again. Feel that emotion gain strength inside your third eye. Feel the shift as you do so. Feel any sensations as you feel the shift, especially in your third eye or on the top of your head.

9. When you are ready, you can also jump a series of notches to the emotion or group of emotions at the Resting Point. Do you want to do that? If okay, continue to step 10. If not, go to Step 19.

10. Look at the chart again. Remember what emotion or group of emotions you are feeling at this moment and where on the chart that emotion or group of emotions resides... Notice which emotion or group of emotions is at the Resting Point of the chart. Say that aloud...

11. Close your eyes. Focusing on the third eye chakra in the middle of your forehead, imagine you can look up through the inside of your head towards the top of your head. Imagine you are taking yourself up an elevator to that more desirable emotion or group of emotions on the chart. Do it now.

12. Feel what it feels like in your third eye, crown chakra, heart and throughout your body. Say the name aloud again…

13. Feel that emotion gain strength inside you. Feel the shift as you do so. Notice any sensations as you feel the shift, especially in your third eye or on the top of your head, although it may be in your throat or heart area. Breathe in the sensations to anchor them…

14. Look at the chart again. Notice which emotion or group of emotions is above the Tipping Point of the chart. You can choose to go up one level at a time or jump any number of steps or go right to the top, which is called Ecstasy. Which emotion or group of emotions would you like to experience?

15. Close your eyes. Focusing on the third eye chakra in the middle of your forehead, imagine you can look up through the inside of your head towards the top of your head. Imagine you are taking yourself up an elevator to that more desirable emotion or group of emotions on the chart.

16. Feel what it feels like in your third eye, crown chakra, heart and throughout your body. Say the name aloud again…

17. Feel that emotion gain strength inside you. Feel the shift as you do so. Notice any sensations as you feel the shift, especially in your third eye or on the top of your head, although it may be anywhere in your body. Breathe in the sensations to anchor them…

You can continue to repeat steps 14-17 as you desire.

18. When you are ready, just for a moment, leave your chair and go look in a mirror to see how you transformed yourself physically as well as emotionally. Then come back and sit down…

19. When you have finished this exercise, take a breath, exhale and relax…

Notebook: Journal your experience.

⁎⁎⁎

Activity: Take down your 6-pointed Lemurian Star. Practice putting it up and taking it down. Practice exercises and meditations while in the Star.

Notebook: What does the Lemurian Star energy feel like? What did you feel when you took down the Lemurian Star? You are learning how to shift energy at will. Write down your experience of this exercise.

⁎⁎⁎

RITUAL GROUP MEDITATION EXERCISE TRAVELING IN YOUR ETHERIC BODY TO MT. SHASTA – EXERCISE #4

This is the time you can practice attending the ritual group meditation as you did at the end of Class #1. Although you may want to skip this exercise, I encourage you to repeat it often as it will stimulate your growth.

Tape recorder or cellphone: You can use a tape recorder or a cellphone to make a recording of the original exercise to or go to YouTube to listen to the descriptions.

Notebook: Journal your experiences when finished.

** Words from the BeeGees

LIVING IN THE NEW LEMURIA:

EXERCISES, PRACTICES, AND TECHNIQUES

Class #6
Words, Beliefs, Focusing

LEMURIAN STAR – MERKABA – SACRED GEOMETRY

Before you begin the next group of exercises in this class, set up your Star. Imagine Gold Light streaming into the Lemurian star. Feel the energy inside. You are learning is to pay close attention to energy and energy shifts and to learn to shift energy at will. Using the 6-pointed Lemurian Star will help increase and change energy when you do exercises in the Star.

Contemplate: What does this energy feel like?

***

Lauren's Law #5: "M = ET²"

This translates to Miracles/Matter/Manifestation/Time .... Equals Energized Thought Squared .... (**Two** or more people)

Miracles of physical matter, events, space, or time can be sped up, increased or transformed through the elevated (spiritual) interaction of two or more people. One person plus one person equals more than two people. Two people plus two people equals MUCH more than four people. The increase of energy is exponential. This is one of the principles of the Lemurian Way and is one main reason why Lemurians worked in groups. Also, we are in the 9th wave of creation from the Mayan Calendar which is about unity.

You may wish to invite your friends to join you in this work as each of you will gain much more than working alone. The learning, growth and evolution of those who study the Lemurian Way in groups of two or more grows in an exponential curve because of the action of $M = ET^2$

You are learning to pay attention to energy and energy shifts. You are learning how to change energy at will. Using the 6-pointed Lemurian Star will help increase and improve energy when you do the exercises within the Star. Utilizing the Rising Above Emotions Exercise #17 that you were introduced to in the last class can also shift your emotions purposefully and deliberately, which also shifts energy. As you shift your energy, you can transform that shift to other people both nearby and far away using energy and mirror neurons.

Lauren's Law #26: "As I transform myself, other people transform themselves in my presence."

"Consciousness is never static or complete... it is an unending process of movement and unfoldment." — David Bohm from the video "Infinite Potential, The Life and Ideas of David Bohm"

Lauren's Law #13: "The Universe is all about Divine Timing. So is everything in your life."

Lauren's Law #20: "Everything is connected to everything as though by an immense Spider Web of Life."

***

VOICE FIGHTING, PART TWO, EXERCISE #18

VOICE FIGHTING is learning how to live in present time, with unconditional love of self, neutrality, acceptance, surrender, and noticing without criticism. What you are learning about thoughts and emotions is that you can notice without judgment; accept; surrender your thoughts and emotions to Creator Source; shift the energy of emotions; and experience neutrality of both thoughts and emotions.

What did you notice about your thoughts and emotions as you did homework during the week? Did thoughts lead to emotions?

Now get out your notebook and turn to your homework page.

If you had emotions of:
>Depression
>Anxiety
>Guilt
>Irrational fear
>Hopelessness
>or Helplessness

Circle those or write them down.

You are learning that your **Voice** recites a script pretending to be you which creates these emotions within you.

Here are the scripts of the 6 Voice Games:

Depression: the **Voice** Game is judgment of self, saying as you: "I'm bad, stupid, worthless, ugly, old, fat, unloved, unloving, etc."

Anxiety: the **Voice** Game is undue apprehension about the future. "What if such and such happens? That would be awful!"

Guilt: The **Voice** Game is about establishing fault and blame of self. "I should; I should not; I hurt people, animals, the world; it's my fault."

Irrational fear: The **Voice** Game is about unnecessary and unreasonable fear of the future. "I will die; I will get a disease; I will faint; I will have a panic attack; I will look and act stupid; I will be alone; I will be homeless or poor."

Hopelessness: The **Voice** Game is about desperation and futility. "I give up; there's no point in going on; the future holds nothing for me; everything in life will continue to be bad."

Helplessness: The **Voice** Game is powerlessness and dependency. "I can't; I'm not able to ...; I'm not strong enough, smart enough, attractive enough, rich enough, powerful enough, popular enough."

Homework assignment #1: During the next week, notice if you feel one of these 6 Voice Game feelings. Without judgment notice the words the Voice is repeating in your mind. Pay attention to what you feel and notice without judgment. Write those feelings and thoughts down.

Homework assignment #1: Listen to the radio, TV, internet and friends' words. There is a not-so-subtle Voice Game the world plays called "Ain't it

Awful." Recognize when the World Voice Game of "Ain't it Awful" is using a script similar to what goes on in your mind. These communications may echo your own Voice which may increase and emphasize your disharmonious thoughts leading to your disharmonious emotions.

Lauren's Law #24: "Pay attention as if your life depends on it. It does."

Lauren's Law #27: "The mind is not my friend."

POWER OF WORDS

We are learning that disharmonious thoughts lead to disharmonious emotions and may result in disharmonious behavior, while helpful thoughts create harmonious emotions that can help us advance spiritually as we learned in the Rising Above Emotions Exercise #17 from Class #5.

Thoughts are made up of individual words. The ancient Egyptian word Hekau means "words of power" which is a reminder that individual words are powerful.

In the mystical Kabbalah from which numerology is derived, each letter connects with a number 1 – 9 each with its own vibration and energy.

A= 1	J= 1	S= 1
B=2	K=2	T=2
C=3	L=3	U=3
D=4	M=4	V=4
E=5	N=5	W=5
F=6	O=6	X=6
G=7	P=7	Y=7
H=8	Q=8	Z=8
I=9	R=9	

Words are formed from numbers which are vibrational.

For example, Lauren – L=3 + A=1 + U=3 + R=9 + E=5 + N=5   Total 27 (add digits 2 + 7) = 9. The vibration of Lauren is 9 in Numerology.

Master numbers are 11, 22, and 33. If you add up a name or word, stop when you get to 11, 22 or 33. [My entire name is a 22. I created that name deliberately, then changed my name legally to Lauren Olea Thyme, a 22, which is a Master Builder Number.]

Lemurians understood the power of words and didn't talk much, while they reserved the potency of words for prayer, chanting and singing. That's much like how many Native Americans view Anglos, often wondering why they talk so much yet say nothing meaningful.

Words can even be expressed physically.

Masuro Emoto is a scientist who performed experiments which showed physically what words do to water. In his book *The Hidden Messages in Water*[1] he documents experiments in which he imbued water with a word, then froze the water. Uplifting words like love, happy, and harmony came out as beautiful snowflakes and other crystalline formations. Negative words like hate, anger, and war — when frozen – created formations which were ugly and non-symmetrical. Dr. Emoto could also take polluted water, imbue the water with a harmonious and uplifting word, which then transformed the water, making it pure.

We humans are made up of mostly water. What do you think words do to us energetically.

We can deliberately choose to focus on harmonious and powerful words, sentences and whole thoughts. When we do this, we shift our energy, attention, and vibration to create what we prefer to have in our lives. This gives us greater power to do, feel and have what we desire,

Here are a few words to contemplate in your daily speech. They can make a difference in what you are trying to convey, even in how you feel.

BUT

Saying the word **but** negates what was said just prior to "but." For example:

> I love you but….
> I am a good person but…
> I am learning fast but…
> I want to do this but….
> I am grateful but…
> I am having fun but….

The "but" negates all the words that came before. You can eliminate the word *BUT* entirely from your conversation and writing and replace it with *AND*.

The word *but* is exclusive, the dividing line between two thoughts into two opposing camps. Whereas the word *and* is inclusive, embracing two thoughts into unified camps.

Feel the difference this makes:

> I love you and…
> I am a good person and…
> I am learning fast and…
> I want to do this and….
> I am grateful and…
> I am having fun and…

Then consider the deadly YEAH… BUT… Have you ever spoken to someone who replied yeah … but … to suggestions you were making? Could you make any headway with that person?

SHOULD

Other words you can examine are should, ought, must, have to, and need to. Can you sense the guilt implicit in these words in the sentences below? Does it sound like the Voice Game of Guilt? Shoulds are not necessary for adults.

> I should be more loving.
> I ought to be helpful.
> I must get my work done.
> I have to be a better person.
> I need to get my hair cut.

These can be replaced by I prefer, I choose, I can, I will, and I am. You can feel the difference.

> I prefer to be more loving.
> I choose to be helpful.
> I can get my work done. I am getting my work done.
> I am a good person.
> I will get my hair cut soon.

A teacher once told me, "Take all your **shoulds** to the **should house."**

TRY

The word Try is another word you can eliminate from your vocabulary if you choose.

Trying … is lying… or, "Just do or don't do", as Yoda says to Luke Skywalker in Star Wars.

For example:
I'll try to do this…
I'm trying…
I'll try to remember…

Instead:

> I'm going to do it.
> I am working on it.
> I will do it.
> I am doing it.
> I will remember. I am remembering.

Exercise: You can use positive statements when you are talking to another person.

> You are doing it.
> You are working on it.
> You are in process.
> You are loveable.
> You are inspiring.

SO FAR

The phrase "so far" can change a thought into a better one, one that might be hopeless into a Hope-Full thought.

> I'm not able to do it… so far.
> I'm sick… so far.
> I'm financially challenged… so far.
> I don't have a partner… so far.

Notebook: Write down any words you want to avoid or focus on in the future.

***

The logical mind became stronger for everyone on the planet when the 7th wave began its activity in 1755 AD. Although the logical mind may not be our friend in all circumstances, we know it is valuable for living, like balancing your checkbook, keeping appointments, and learning new information.

Although the mind may not be our friend for emotional and spiritual improvement, the mind can be joined with the spiritual heart for discernment on our spiritual journey. According to the book *HeartMath* by Doc Childre and *Resilience of the Heart* by Gregg Braden, the heart, rather than the mind itself, is a coherent source of wisdom. Ancient Egyptians believed the heart was the seat of wisdom. When mummifying a corpse, they removed the brain through the nose and threw it away. Then they removed the heart, mummified it, and finally returned the heart to the mummified body to be entombed together forever.

Scientists are now discovering that the **gut** has a mind all its own where microbes [the microbiome] can control the thoughts, feelings and physical health of a person. We have more microbial DNA in our body than human DNA. The biggest collection of the human body's 100 trillion microbes is in our gut. What is a human being anyway?

The phrase "gut feeling" then takes on a whole new meaning and is connected to discernment.

***

JUDGMENT and the BATTLE OF BELIEFS

Read and contemplate my essay "The Battle Of Beliefs" below. The Battle of Beliefs started with the 6th wave of the Mayan Calendar, which also includes the Hologram of Good and Evil. Us versus them. Judgment and polarity on this planet lead to unpleasant consequences in relationships, countries, and the world.

The Mystic Rumi wrote, "Out beyond ideas of wrongdoing and right doing there is a field. I'll meet you there."

In the 9th wave of the Mayan calendar which began in 2011, there is only US.

Now that we are in the 9th wave of Creation, Lemurians include all of us — even those who don't remember, didn't incarnate or may not believe in Lemuria. I call us The New Lemurians. You can translate that to "spiritually inclined."

BATTLE OF BELIEFS

I often have felt like George Carlin who said (I'm paraphrasing) "I don't feel like a member of the human species. I feel connected to protons and atoms, though…"

What is it that makes me feel separate?

When it appears the world is going to "hell in a hand-basket," why don't people believe what I tell them about what we can do? I feel alone on a street corner, holding a sign that proclaims, "Pay Attention!" and what's worse is I seem like some nutcase. Chicken Little. The sky is falling. "Look," I beg them, "here's a piece of the sky. It fell down yesterday…"

But then, on the opposite spectrum, I warn of impending miracles. We can make a change in consciousness. One person can make a difference. Together we can help our beautiful earth recover, endure, and heal. Our species can survive, along with all the other wonderful species we're joined with.

What makes me feel as though I'm "blowing in the wind" as Bob Dylan sang?

I think it's because the main war on this planet seems to be a Battle of Beliefs.

> Christian versus Muslim versus Jew versus Hindu versus atheist versus pagan.
> Conservative versus Liberal versus Green versus save-the-whales versus save-the-corporations.

MSNBC versus Fox News versus The Daily Show versus web-
sites.

Female versus male versus transsexual.

Young versus old.

Conservation versus keeping-all-your-lights-burning.

Rich versus poor.

Name brand versus thrift store.

Organic versus agri-business.

Us versus them.

It's worse than that. We're having a Tower of Babel convergence of Beliefs – a Bottleneck of Beliefs, a Bombardment of Beliefs, with so many people simul-taneously saying so many different things, it's dizzying and confusing.

What's true? What's not?

"My belief is better than your belief.

"My belief is real. Yours is shit."

"You must be crazy to believe like that."

"You'll go to hell if you believe in that."

"You'll go to heaven if you believe in this."

"You'll be miserable if you believe in that."

"You'll be happy if you buy this."

"You're doomed if you don't believe this."

The Battle of Beliefs makes ordinary people, nations, neighbors and families into enemies. Enemies are dehumanized individuals who are easy to devalue, push to the sidelines, even murder. What about Black Lives Matter? What do many Americans think of Iraqis and Afghanis? Or Middle Easterners or Mus-lims? Remember Bosnia and "ethnic cleansing?" How do Israelis think of Palestinians? How about Rwanda, where the Hutus regarded the Tutsis as cockroaches. How difficult is it to squash a cockroach?

…and what if all feelings and thoughts and beliefs are created equal?

What if nobody's wrong?

What if everyone's right?!

That would be a relief.

What if each of us lives in our own separate reality? In this reality, a separate Universe that each of us inhabits, everything is true and correct and real.

That means….

> I can believe in a horrible collapse of our civilization and I'm right,
>
> Or
>
> I can believe we are creating a wonderful, miraculous shift into a golden age and I'm still right.

Which reality do I choose to live in? Do I straddle the fence? Weighing my options? Hedging my bets?

That means that no matter what a person says to me, I can simply reply, "You're right." Is that mind-blowing? Can I do it? Do I need to do it?

That means that:

> Mother Theresa was right. Saddam Hussein was right. G.W. Bush was right. Gandhi was right.
> Trump is right. Biden is right. Putin is right. Greta Thunberg is right.

You get the idea.

That means that all my enemies and all my friends — and all those 7.8 billion people I don't even know — are right.

That means I don't have to fight over, argue, or debate anything. I don't have to fight my own Battle of Beliefs. I'm not better than you. I'm not better – or worse – than anyone. I am purely, simply, distinctly *equal*. The same as everyone. Existing in my own wonderful (or awful) universe, as each person lives in his or hers. Whatever my universe is, I'm right.

That means that peace exists out beyond the field of battle. In the verdant meadow beyond the Battle of Beliefs lies peaceful co-existence. Co-operation. Harmony. Community. Oneness. Absolute equality.

Scientists and quantum physicists including David Bohm have concluded that "everything is connected to everything." Many ancient religions and spiritual traditions concur. That means that even if I *believe* I'm *separate* from everyone, every event, every blessing, every awful tragedy, I'm not. My personal universe is connected, invisibly and *attached to* every other personal universe, whether I want to be or not, whether I like it or not.

That puts a different spin on my world. The "blame game" comes to an end. There is no one to blame for the world's problems: climate change, pollution of water, earth and air, too many people, too much money and power in a few hands, or economic collapse. "Somebody else will fix those problems," I can say. "It's not my worry."

If everything is connected to everything, while I live in my own Universe of beliefs, then the only one to hold responsible (*not guilty*) in my Universe — is me. The only one who can fix my Universe is me. The only one who can alter my beliefs is me. Changing my beliefs can change my universe. Changing my beliefs **does** change my universe. I've tried it, and experienced miracles. Miracles live in a peaceful pasture outside the Battle of Beliefs."

Excerpt from *Cosmic Grandma Wisdom* © 2017 Lauren O. Thyme
Originally posted at *galdepress.com* April 2014

Notebook: Write down any thoughts or feelings you have after reading this essay.

***

BABAJI MEDITATION

When I was 23, a new Elder popped in to replace the Chinese Elder Yuan who had been working with me since I was 15. The new Elder started teaching me every day. I didn't know who he was but could see his image, hear his words, and feel him. A few months later a friend of mine loaned me *Autobiography of a Yogi* by Paramahansa Yogananda. As I looked through the pictures, I found a picture of him: The Elder. Babaji. I could hardly believe Babaji was coming to me because I was nobody special.

When I asked him why he was showing up to teach me, he replied with a simple answer. "Because you listen." He's been with me ever since, along with 7 others, whom I call Lemurian Elders, since they had physical incarnations in the ancient land of Lemuria.

Two great teachings from Babaji are his instructions on Meditation and Lucid Dreaming, which I never forgot, although that was 49 years ago. These were unlike anything I'd ever heard of or tried before or since.

Instead of emptying one's mind, Babaji instructs you to sharply focus your attention instead, as you did with your Pieces of Gold Light Wisdom mantra chant. Focusing on the 5 senses also teaches you the Extra-Senses of clairvoyance, clairaudience, clairsentience, clairalience, and clairgustance so that you may become more proficient in "paying attention" to extrasensory perception.

BABAJI MEDITATION PRACTICE – EXERCISE #19

HOMEWORK Assignment: Get out your **notebook** and open to a new page.

Write these instructions: "Do the Babaji meditation steps 1 through 8, one step per day."

Step 1:

Get comfortable in a quiet setting with no distractions. This exercise is best done late at night.

Close your eyes and relax. Slowly breathe in and out for 3 breaths. Next review your day starting from the beginning. Remember everything of importance that happened today, whether you liked it or not.

Focus on those events you would like to repeat and which ones you'd like to change. Would you want to repeat it? Would you want to share it with others? How did the event feel? Did it have a taste, a smell, a vision? How would you use that event in your future? Or would you want to avoid it at all costs? Take a deep breath and release the event. You don't have to DO anything except avoid judging yourself. Simply focus and then release.

When you're ready, pick a simple object — an orange. Imagine you are holding it in your hand.

Smell it, feel it, and look at it as though you had never before seen an orange. Say the name aloud: "Orange."

Then pull it open to find the orange inside and proceed to pull the segments apart.

Feel the juice dripping through your fingers. Smell it. Taste it on your fingers.

Look at it intently. See the orange color. The white membrane. The seeds. Remove the seeds with your fingers. Squeeze a segment.

In other words, completely experience the "orange."

Finally release the "orange" and free it from your awareness. Let it go. Breathe.

Relax.

Wait at least 24 hours before doing next step.

Step 2:

Get comfortable in a quiet setting with no distractions. Slowly and deeply breathe in and out for about 3-4 breaths, close your eyes, and relax.

Review your day starting from the beginning. Remember everything of importance that happened that day, whether you liked it or not.

Focus on those events you would like to repeat and which ones you'd like to change. Would you want to repeat it? Would you want to share it with others? How did the event feel? Did it have a taste, a smell, a vision? How would you use that event in your future? Would you want to avoid it at all costs? Take a deep breath and release the event. You don't have to **DO** anything except avoid judging yourself. Simply focus and then release.

Pick another simple object which has a function—a wooden pencil. Smell it, feel it, and look at it as though you have never before seen a leaded pencil. Say the name, "Pencil." Take a pencil sharpener and sharpen it. "Smell that," Feel the point. Feel the eraser. Feel the wooden edges. Can you lick it with your tongue and taste it? Does it have a distinctive taste and feel to your tongue? Next use it the way "pencil" would be used. Write with it. Print with it. Erase the words with the eraser. Break the leaded point. What does that broken point feel like? Does it have a different taste, texture and smell? Does breaking the pencil bring up any feelings in you?

Then release all of the "pencil" and let it go from your awareness, watching it disappear. Breathe. Relax.

Wait at least 24 hours before doing the next step.

Step 3:

Get comfortable in a quiet setting with no distractions.

Slowly and deeply breathe in and out for about 3-4 breaths, close your eyes, and relax. Review your day starting from the beginning. Remember everything of importance that happened that day, whether you liked it or not.

Focus on those events you would like to repeat and which ones you'd like to change. Would you want to repeat it? Would you want to share it with others? How did the event feel? Did it have a taste, a smell, a vision? How would you use that event in your future? Would you want to avoid it at all costs? Take a deep breath and release the event. You don't have to **DO** anything except avoid judging yourself. Simply focus and then release.

Next select a simple word, one which would not bring up any issues or complex thoughts or emotions, like **walk.**

What does this word mean to you? Smell the word. Taste it. Feel it. See it. Hear it. Does it have a sound when you say the word? Does it have a feeling when you say the word? Use the word in a simple sentence, in context. Then another sentence. Then another. Can you feel the sentence? Turn the word over and over, exploring and examining it. How does it feel on your lips and tongue to say the word? Make the word yours. Own it.

Then release the word and let it go from your awareness, watch it disappear. Breathe. Relax.

Wait at least 24 hours before doing the next step.

Step 4:

Get comfortable in a quiet setting with no distractions. Slowly and deeply breathe in and out for about 3-4 breaths, close your eyes, and relax. Review your day starting from the beginning. Remember everything of importance that happened that day, whether you liked it or not.

Focus on those events you would like to repeat and which ones you'd like to change. Would you want to repeat it? Would you want to share it with others? How did the event feel? Did it have a taste, a smell, a vision? How would you use that event in your future? Would you want to avoid it at all costs? Take a deep breath and release the event. You don't have to **DO** anything except avoid judging yourself. Simply focus and then release.

Next select a word that has meaning for you, and refrain from triggering words like love, hate, god, sex, death, or birth. *Care* might be a good word to practice with.

Do the same thing with the new, more complex word. What does it mean to you? Smell it. Taste it. Feel it. See it. Hear it. Does it have a sound when you say the word? Does it have a feeling when you say the word? Use the word in a simple sentence, in context. Then another sentence. Then another. Can you feel the sentence? Turn the word over and over, exploring and examining it. How does it feel on your lips and tongue to say the word? Make the word yours. Own it.

Then release the word and let it go from your awareness, watching it disappear. Breathe. Relax.

Wait at least 24 hours before doing next step.

Step 5:

Get comfortable in a quiet setting with no distractions. Slowly and deeply breathe in and out for about 3-4 breaths, close your eyes, and relax.

Review your day starting from the beginning. Remember everything of importance that happened that day, whether you liked it or not.

Focus on those events you would like to repeat and which ones you'd like to change. Would you want to repeat it? Would you want to share it with others? How did the event feel? Did it have a taste, a smell, a vision? How would you use that event in your future? Would you want to avoid it at all costs? Take a deep breath and release the event. You don't have to **DO** anything except avoid judging yourself. Simply focus and then release.

Next select a word that has a lot of meaning, such as love, hate, god, sex, death, or birth.

Do the same thing with the new, more complex word. Smell it. Taste it. Feel it. See it. Hear it. Does it have a sound when you say the word? Does it have a feeling when you say the word? Use the word in a simple sentence, in context. Then another sentence. Then another. Can you feel the sentence? Turn the word over and over, exploring and examining it. How does it feel on your lips and tongue to say the word? How does it feel in your body? Make the word yours. Own it.

Be aware of the multiple meanings and depth of feelings of that word. Just notice.

Then release the word and let it go from your awareness, watching it disappear. Breathe. Relax.

Wait at least 24 hours before doing next step.

Step 6:

Get comfortable in a quiet setting with no distractions.

Deeply breathe in and out for about 3-4 breaths, close your eyes, and relax. Review your day starting from the beginning. Remember everything of importance that happened that day, whether you liked it or not.

This time choose an event earlier in your day that you ***liked a lot.*** Would you want to repeat it? Would you want to share it with others? How did the event feel? Did it have a taste, a smell, a vision? How would you use that event in your future? Take a deep breath and release the event.

Next pick any object, any word, any phrase and do the same thing you have been practicing. "Smell, taste, touch, see, and hear." You understand how to do the exercise by now. Do *not* choose a person.

Release whatever you had chosen and let it go from your awareness, watching it disappear. Breathe. Relax.

Wait at least 24 hours before doing next step.

Step 7:

Get comfortable in a quiet setting with no distractions. Slowly and deeply breathe in and out for about 3-4 breaths, close your eyes, and relax.

"Review your day starting from the beginning. Remember everything of importance that happened that day, whether you liked it or not."

Choose an event earlier in your day that you ***didn't like*** which made you uncomfortable or even emotional, or hurt someone, or someone hurt you. Would you want to repeat it? Would you want to share it with others? How did the event feel? Did it have a taste, a smell, a look? How would you use that event in your future? *Would* you use it in your future? How could you change that event into one that felt good? Do you want to do that? If you hurt someone, could you apologize? If so, imagine yourself apologizing. If someone hurt you, could you forgive that person? You can imagine yourself forgiving.

Take a deep breath, relax and release the event.

Next pick any object, word, or phrase and do the same thing you have been practicing. Do *not* choose a person. "Smell, taste, touch, see, and hear." You understand how to do the exercise by now.

Release whatever you had chosen and let it go from your awareness, watching it disappear. Breathe. Relax.

Then take a deep breath, relax and release whatever you have chosen.

Wait at least 24 hours before taking the next step.

Step 8:

Get comfortable in a quiet setting with no distractions. Slowly and deeply breathe in and out for about 3-4 breaths, close your eyes, and relax.

Review your day starting from the beginning. Remember everything of importance that happened that day, whether you liked it or not.

Choose to review an event from the day, pleasant or unpleasant, and do the instructions from Step 6 or Step 7 above.

Take a deep breath, relax and release everything.

Then choose an object, simple or complicated, or a word, or a phrase, simple or complicated. "Feel. See. Hear. Smell. Taste." You can include a person.

Next pick a second object, word, or phrase and do the same thing. Smell, taste, touch, see, and hear. Use it in context. Take it apart and put it back together. You know how to do the exercise by now. You can include a person.

Then take a deep breath, relax and release whatever you have chosen.

After Step 8, you can practice these steps every day, especially if you are feeling disharmonious emotions and feelings or want to review pleasant or unpleasant events.

Notebook: Keep a journal of your experiences.

***

RITUAL GROUP MEDITATION EXERCISE TRAVELING IN YOUR ETHERIC BODY TO MT. SHASTA – EXERCISE #4

This is the time you can practice attending the ritual group meditation as you did at the end of Class #1. Although you may want to skip this exercise, I encourage you to repeat it often as it will stimulate your growth.

Tape recorder or cellphone: You can use a tape recorder or a cellphone to make a recording of the original exercise to or go to YouTube to listen to the descriptions.

Notebook: Journal your experiences when finished.

***

If you have questions or concerns, you may send me an email at *thyme.lauren@gmail.com.*

**

At this point you may "take down"—remove—your Lemurian 6-pointed star formation. As you do so, pay attention to discerning an energy shift. Can you feel the difference?

Notebook: Write down any experiences, insights and transformations you had. Write down your experiences with the Lemurian Star.

The Hidden Messages in Water, Masuro Emoto
The Heartmath Solution, Doc Childre
Resilience from the Heart, Gregg Braden

LIVING IN THE NEW LEMURIA:

EXERCISES, PRACTICES, AND TECHNIQUES

Class #7
Protection, Face of God, Lucid Dreaming

***

LEMURIAN STAR – MERKABA – SACRED GEOMETRY

Contemplate: Set up your Lemurian Star. What does this energy feel like?

Notebook: Write down your observations.

IN THE BEGINNING
In the beginning before beginnings was the void.
Out of the void came the Light.
The Light was called Love and it was good.
All things come from the Light, and will return to the Light, and can bask in the Light.
Light is Love,
and Love is all-illuminating.
So let us start upon the road to realizing **WE** are the light.
– Lauren O. Thyme 1971, excerpt *from Cosmic Grandma Wisdom © 2017*

Lauren's Law #2: "Love is the building block of the universe, from which everything emanates."

Lauren's Law #26: "As I transform myself, other people transform themselves in my presence." "In my presence" can mean directly next to someone or dynamically across the planet.

CREATOR SOURCE SAFETY AND PROTECTION — EXERCISE #20

Steps: Imagine that Creator Source is floating above you in a giant warm bubble of gold light.

Ask Creator Source to send Gold Light Blessings into your body through the top of your head. Feel the gold light warmth and peaceful flow as it enters you. Allow it to radiate throughout your head, into your body, arms, legs and feet, then into the ground below you. Deeply breathe again and feel the blessings you are receiving from Creator Source.

Get out your Creator Source Container and some slips of paper.

On the first slip of paper write your full name. Place it gently in your Creator Source Container and put your hand over the container.

Take a breath. Say the following words aloud:

> **I (say your full name),**
> am now safe and protected by Creator Source
> with Gold Light Blessings entering me,
> filling me with absolute health and well-being
> in body, mind, emotions, relationships and spirit.
> Thank you, Creator Source.

Take a breath.

On the 2nd slip of paper write "All the members of my family."

Place the slip gently in your Creator Source Container and put your hand over the container.

Take a breath. Relax.

Say the following words aloud:

> "All the members of my family
> are now safe and protected by Creator Source
> as Gold Light Blessings enter them,
> filling them with absolute health and well-being
> in body, mind, emotions, relationships and spirit."
> Thank you, Creator Source.

> Take a breath and relax.

On the 3rd slip of paper write "All the members of my city – (name your city).

Place the slip gently in your Creator Source Container and put your hand over the container.

Take a breath and relax.

Say the following words aloud:

> "All the members of my city … (name your city)
> are now safe and protected by Creator Source
> as Gold Light Blessings enter them,
> filling them with absolute health and well-being
> in body, mind, emotions, relationships and spirit."
> Thank you, Creator Source.

> Take a breath.

On the 4th slip of paper write "All the members of my country... (name your country).

Place the slip gently in your Creator Source Container and put your hand over the container.

Take a breath. Relax.

Say the following words aloud:

> "All the members of my country … (name your country)
> are now safe and protected by Creator Source
> as Gold Light Blessings enter them,
> filling them with absolute health and well-being
> in body, mind, emotions, relationships and spirit."
> Thank you, Creator Source.

Take a breath.

On the 5th slip of paper write "All the members of planet Earth"

Place the slip gently in your Creator Source Container and put your hand over the container.

Take a deep breath. Relax.

Say the following words aloud:

> "All the members of Planet Earth
> are now safe and protected by Creator Source
> as Gold Light Blessings enter them,
> filling them with absolute health and well-being
> in body, mind, emotions, relationships and spirit."
> Thank you, Creator Source.

Take a breath and relax.

On the 6th slip of paper write "All the plants, animals, lands, oceans, seas, lakes, rivers, and air of planet Earth"

Place the slip gently in your Creator Source Container and put your hand over the container.

Take a deep breath. Relax.

Say the following words aloud:

> "All the plants, animals, lands, oceans, seas, lakes and rivers
> and air of planet Earth
> are now safe and protected by Creator Source
> as Gold Light Blessings surround them,
> supplying them with absolute health and well-being."
> Thank you, Creator Source.

Take your hand off your Creator Source container, release and relax. Open your eyes. Feel the chair you are sitting in. Feel your feet on the floor. Come back into present time. Breathe…

∗∗∗

The Mayans formulated a calendar that explained evolution from the Big Bang to today and beyond, including the elaborate and intricate timing of the 9 waves of creation. Many cultures and civilizations have had stories, myths, and sacred writing to explain what the Universe is, how it came into being, and how we humans fit into it, including stories and imagery of the Tree of Life.

The Mayans believed the Big Bang was created from the Tree of Life. Did that originate in the mind of Creator Source?

"The cosmic Tree of Life is not a thing made out of matter. Rather, it is the geometric source of the space-time through which the matter of the universe is organized."[1]

LEMURIAN 6-POINTED STAR – MERKABA – SACRED GEOMETRY

Why do we work with the Lemurian Star, as did the ancient Lemurians? Because the Universe is based on Sacred Geometry, as the Lemurians intuited, who used the Star and their Gold Light Pyramid in their daily existence.

"Geometry existed before the Creation. It is co-eternal with the mind of God…Geometry is God itself." Johannes Kepler, *Harmonices Mundi* (1618 CE)

From the instant of creation everything in our Universe is thereby connected to everything, progressing from light, nebulae, stars, planets, to our planet Earth, then evolving from molecules to single-cell organisms, reptiles, mammals and finally us. **We** are the Light of the Big Bang. **We are star dust**. Each of us is connected from a common source, *as connected to each other*, the planet Earth, animals, insects, mammals, reptiles and amphibians. Unity in Harmony connected to Creator Source and Conscious Co-Creation is the last essential, ultimate step in our long evolution, the 9th Wave, which began in 2011 CE.

The 9 waves of creation are part of our own progression as humans, coming to us from the Big Bang, through 200,000 years of countless generations, through our DNA and memories. We correspond to the on-going creation of the universe through our own lives. Each of us, from conception through adulthood, start as a tiny dot of life, egg and sperm, coming together, then growing into an embryo, a fetus, birthing as an infant, maturing into adulthood and ultimately wisdom.

"The point is to use the Ninth Wave in such a way that you yourself become aware of how your life can become part of the destiny of humanity...[2] [and] rid yourself of all the negative effects of the dualities created by the lower [waves]."[3]

We all came from one Source. We went through various stages of evolution and consciousness, developing certain abilities and expanding understanding, similar to children in school going through kindergarten, elementary, high school and university. Now we are in the final 9th wave stage of understanding, yet confused because of old teachings that are no longer relevant, especially from waves 6 through 8. Those former dominant concepts and modes of living were applicable then yet now outmoded, even archaic, no longer serving the purpose of our evolutionary development. Also, because we are in a valley instead of a peak, we experience a dark time. Now more than ever, the Lemurian Way can help us navigate this challenging period through simple lessons of Gold Light Wisdom and exercises meant to embody those concepts by working with others who wish to do the same. Because Creator Source created our Universe, including Planet Earth, the health of our bodies, minds, hearts, souls and relationships must be organic. In other words, health stemming from and resonating with the Divine Plan.

What happens when we eat food that is artificially grown with chemicals? **Dis-ease.**

What happens when we treat ourselves and others in ways that are not aligned with Gold Light Wisdom? **Dis-harmony.**

According to the Mayan calendar, in 2011 as the 9th Wave began, we entered a dark valley, as the 6th, 7th, and 8th waves moved from Day into Night. The 6th wave will turn into day in 2406 CE while the 7th wave will turn into day in 2031 CE. We have time to do our work. Thus, it is up to each of you to navigate the Night by being the "best self" you can be. Rather than being the problem, you can instead choose to be the solution. This choice does **not** include lecturing, arguing or evangelizing. It *does* include what Mahatma Gandhi (Great Soul) said, "to **BE** the change we wish to see in the world."

We do not need to focus on challenges coming from the Divine Plan. We can instead focus on solutions and then model those while working in harmony with others, thus creating the *Maharishi Effect* of exponential positive change.

Lauren's Law #5: "M = ET²" Miracles equal 2 or more people coming together and sharing in energized (spiritual) thought.

Scientists are discovering that evolution comes from cooperation. The strongest person doesn't necessarily win. Are the "survival of the fittest" the ones most able to adapt to the demands of the times? Perhaps we can live in the "survival of the **finest**."

FACE OF GOD

The philosopher Martin Heidegger said, "A person is not a thing or a process but an opening through which the Absolute can manifest."

25 years ago, when the Elders gave me this exercise out of the blue, they said, "We want you to go to Homeless Park [in the city I was living in]. We want to show you something." I was frightened because Homeless Park was a place where junkies, prostitutes, gang members and other desperate people hung out.

When I got there the Elders said to me, "Sit on this bench." They said, "Look at all the different faces and see the face of God in each of them." I sat and practiced.

The most dramatic face belonged to a disheveled woman, obviously very drunk, reeking of alcohol, with filthy hair, tattered clothing, and recent knife cuts all over her face. She sat down on the bench next to me, speaking incoherently. We sat together as I practiced until I saw her face transform into the Face of God. It still brings me to tears to remember it.

Since we are each a component of the Divine Plan, people are all Divine **re-**

gardless of how a person **looks and acts**. Healing planetary consciousness takes courageous steps. An important step is to be able to see the face of God everywhere.

FACE OF GOD – EXERCISE #21

Before you start the exercise, take out your notebook, open to a new page and write these words, "Over the next week, I will practice observing faces on TV, the internet, or while in public (like while shopping) and see each face as the Face of God."

If you wish, you can also think of a person that you have difficulty with and practice this exercise while visualizing that person.

Gaze upon a person while concentrating on seeing the Face of God, Creator Source, or however you name the Divine. Some faces may be easy to contemplate as the Face of God while others may be difficult. Simply *notice* if judgement comes up. If judgment happens keep repeating to yourself, "This is the Face of God" until you notice a shift, no matter how slight. Examples might include Jesus of Nazareth, Mother Teresa, Adolph Hitler, Mahatma Gandhi, Martin Luther King Jr., different races than your own, tattooed or pierced individuals, soldiers from countries other than your own, a politician, a little child, a homeless person, and so on. Be creative to stretch your spiritual muscles.

Notebook: Keep a journal of this exercise.

VOICE FIGHTING REVISITED – EXERCISE #22

The Voice is an internalized voice based on what you have heard and believed throughout your life, from parents, family, teachers, playmates, friends, partners and the world around you. The Voice may even be related to other lifetimes. Freud labeled the voice as coming from the ego or the superego.

Take out your notebook. What thoughts and emotions did you notice during the past week? Did the Voice play any Games with you during the week? Circle those.

Assignment: Create six 3"x 5" index cards or find these at an office supply store.

On each card, using the information from this script, write or type/print each Voice Game, (e.g., Depression), what the Voice says and responses to the Voice. You will do one Voice game per card, for a total of 6 cards. You can also write your own responses.

You will take these cards with you wherever you go. You will refer to the appropriate card when you notice the voice giving its unpleasant commentary and/or you are feeling the emotion. Identify the emotion, take out the corresponding card, and respond to the voice aloud.

For example, Guilt, "I should", you respond "Voice, there are no rules about what I should or shouldn't do. **I** decide." And so on. Do as many of the responses as you desire in whatever order you want. You can also make up your own responses. You, not the voice, are the boss.

If, after going through the responses and the Voice persists, you can say, "Voice, back off!! Get away!! Stop bothering me!!" Then proceed to ignore it by doing a simple activity like washing dishes, taking a walk, or petting your dog.

In time, with practice, you will notice the Voice will play its games less frequently and less intensely.

You may notice with practice the Voice will disappear just by you noticing it. Now here is each Voice Game with constructive responses to "fight" the games the **VOICE** may play with you.

Depression Game: *the* **Voice** *says (as you),* *"I'm bad, stupid, worthless, ugly, old, fat, unloved, unloving, etc."*

Your constructive response:

> Voice, I am a good, loving, and worthwhile person.

> Voice, I have friends and people all over the world who love and like me.

> Voice, what you tell me is hurtful and I don't have to pay attention.

> Voice, it's only when I listen to you that I feel depressed.

> Voice, I don't have to listen to what you tell me. You are a liar.

> Voice, I can choose who I want to be with.

> Voice, I'm ignoring you now.

> Voice, back off!! Go away!! Stop bothering me!!

Anxiety Game: *the* **Voice** *declares undue apprehension about the future:* *"What if such and such happens? That would be awful!"*

Your constructive response:

> Voice, there are no what ifs in life. That is a myth.

> Voice, I don't have to worry about something that hasn't happened yet.

> Voice, it is only you who gives me ideas about being worried about the future.

Voice, the future will take care of itself. Whatever happens will not be awful.

Voice, facts about the future do not exist except in the words you put in my head.

Voice, I am creating my own positive future.

Voice, I'm ignoring you now.

Voice, back off!! Go away!! Stop bothering me!!

Guilt Game: *the **Voice** tries to establish fault and blame of self. "I should; I should not; I hurt people, animals, the world; it's my fault."*

Your constructive response:

Voice, there are no rules about what I should or shouldn't do. I decide.

Voice, I don't hurt people on purpose.

Voice, if I hurt someone, I can apologize or make amends.

Voice, I take care of myself first and that is a good thing.

Voice, I am not responsible for other people's lives (or the world).

Voice, it is only you who makes me feel guilty.

Voice, I'm ignoring you now.

Voice, back off!! Go away!! Stop bothering me!!

Irrational Fear Game: *the Voice brings up unnecessary and unreasonable fears of the future: "I will die; I will get a disease; I will faint; I will have a panic attack; I will look and act stupid; I will be alone; I will be homeless or poor."* Your constructive response:

Voice, I am safe in the world, in my body, and out in public.

Voice, I am safe, secure and healthy in my life.

Voice, I have friends and other people in my life.

Voice, I can choose what I want and whom I want in my life.

Voice, there is no logical reason to believe I will be homeless or poor.

Voice, you are scaring me, and I don't have to believe what you say.

Voice, I'm ignoring you now.

Voice, back off!! Go away!! Stop bothering me!!

Hopelessness Game: *the Voice whines about desperation and futility. "I give up; there's no point in going on; the future holds nothing for me; everything in life will continue to be bad."*

Your constructive response:

Voice, I am strong and able to live my life the way I choose.

Voice, I am creating a positive future for myself.

Voice, no matter what is happening, I will prevail.

Voice, the future is based on how I live today, not what you tell me.

Voice, it is only you trying to convince me that my life is hopeless.

Voice, there are no hard facts to demonstrate that my life is hopeless.

Voice, I'm ignoring you now.

Voice, back off!! Go away!! Stop bothering me!!

Helplessness Game: *the* **Voice** *warns of powerlessness and dependency. "I can't; I'm not able to ...; I'm not strong enough, smart enough, attractive enough, rich enough, powerful enough, popular enough."*

Your constructive response:

Voice, I am strong and smart, able to take care of my life in a positive way.

Voice, whatever happened in the past does not make me helpless in the present or future.

Voice, no matter what my challenges are, I will persevere.
Voice, I can and I will live my life expecting miracles.

Voice, it is only you who tells me I cannot do anything.

Voice, I have been able to accomplish things in the past.

Voice, there are no facts about what I can and cannot do.

Voice, I'm ignoring you now.

Voice, back off!! Go away!! Stop bothering me!!

Notebook: Journal your experiences with the Voice Games.

BABAJI'S LUCID DREAMING

Babaji shared Lucid Dreaming exercises with me 50 years ago, which I practiced for many years. I shared this exercise for the first time in my self-help book *Catherine, Karma and Complex PTSD*. This series of exercises is intended to help you become more aware of your life through your dream state, to actively participate in changing your subconscious, which in turn transforms your consciousness and generates more power and peace for you.

Lucid dreaming, like most dreams, usually happens during **REM (rapid eye movement) sleep.** In a lucid dream, you **know** that you're dreaming. You're **aware** of your awareness during the dream state. About 55% of people have experienced one or more lucid dreams in their lifetime.

To have good REM sleep:

Follow a sleep schedule.
Exercise daily.
Avoid electronics including cellphones at least an hour before bed.
Create a relaxing sleep environment.
Avoid caffeine and alcohol before bed.

This process takes patience and persistence. You may achieve lucid dreaming quickly or it may take time. You are training your consciousness, which is designed to follow your instructions. This exercise works better once you have practiced the Babaji Meditation exercises from Class #6.

Notebook: Get out your notebook, turn to a new page and write these instructions:

"I will follow the instructions for Lucid Dreaming for nights 1 through 9."

You may also wish to continue after 9 nights.

BABAJI'S LUCID DREAMING – EXERCISE #23

Night 1:

Keep a special notepad with a writing instrument *close by* to make notes when you wake up. This will be your dream notebook.

Get comfortable in a quiet setting with no distractions, preferably *just before* going to sleep. A warm bath beforehand or some gentle stretching may be helpful.

Slowly and deeply breathe in and out for about 3-4 breaths, close your eyes, and relax.

Review your day starting from the beginning. Remember everything of importance that happened that day, whether you liked it or not. Remember. Focus. Release.

Next, say out loud: **"I am going to have one dream tonight and I will remember it when I wake up."** Breathe. Relax. Repeat that phrase 4-5 times. Breathe. Relax.

Then go to sleep.

If you need to keep breathing rhythmically and relaxing for a while to help you go to sleep, please do so.

When you wake up (either in the middle of the night or in the morning), write down any dream you can remember. Even if it is just a few words. An image. A feeling.

Night 2:

Keep a special notepad with a writing instrument *close by* to make notes for when you wake up. This will be your dream notebook.

Get comfortable in a quiet setting with no distractions, preferably *just before* going to sleep. A warm bath beforehand or some gentle stretching may be helpful.

Slowly and deeply breathe in and out for about 3-4 breaths, close your eyes, and relax.

Review your day starting from the beginning. Remember everything of importance that happened that day, whether you liked it or not. Remember. Focus. Release."

Next say aloud, **"I am going to have one dream tonight and I will remember it when I wake up."** Breathe. Relax.

Repeat that phrase 4-5 times. Breathe. Relax.

Then go to sleep.

If you need to keep rhythmically breathing and relaxing for a while to help you go to sleep, please do so.

When you wake up (either in the middle of the night or in the morning), write down any dream you can remember. Even if it is just a few words. An image. A feeling.

Night 3:

Keep a special notepad with a writing instrument close by to make notes for when you wake up. This will be your dream notebook.

Get comfortable in a quiet setting with no distractions, preferably *just before* going to sleep. A warm bath beforehand or some gentle stretching may be helpful.

Slowly and deeply breathe in and out for about 3-4 breaths, close your eyes, and relax.

Review your day starting from the beginning. Remember everything of importance that happened that day, whether you liked it or not. Remember. Focus. Release.

Next say aloud, **"I am going to have one dream tonight and I will remember it when I wake up."** Breathe. Relax.

Repeat that phrase 4-5 times. Breathe. Relax.

Then go to sleep.

If you need to keep rhythmically breathing and relaxing for a while to help you go to sleep, please do so.

When you wake up (either in the middle of the night or in the morning), write down any dream you can remember. Even if it is just a few words. An image. A feeling.

Night 4: Getting Lucid

Keep a special notepad with a writing instrument close by to make notes for when you wake up. This will be your dream notebook.

Get comfortable in a quiet setting with no distractions, preferably *just before* going to sleep. A warm bath beforehand may be helpful.

Slowly and deeply breathe in and out for about 3-4 breaths, close your eyes, and relax.

Review your day starting from the beginning. Remember everything of importance that happened that day, whether you liked it or not. Remember. Focus. Release.

Next say aloud, "**I am going to have one dream tonight and I will become aware** *as I'm dreaming it.*" Breathe. Relax.

Repeat that phrase 4-5 times. Breathe. Relax.

Then go to sleep.

If you need to keep breathing and relaxing for a while to help you go to sleep, please do so.

A lucid dream happens when you are dreaming yet conscious you are dreaming. When you become aware you are lucid while dreaming, pay close attention. Look at your hand. Look around. Do items shift as you look around? Is anything happening? Are any persons there with you? What are your surroundings? Notice everything.

When you are done with the lucid dream *wake up and write down* that dream in your dream notebook. Even if it is just a few words. An image. A feeling.

When you wake up again (either in the middle of the night or in the morning), write down any other dream you can remember in your dream notebook. Even if it is just a few words. An image. A feeling.

Nights 5, 6 and so on – deepening your lucid dreaming:

Keep a special notepad with a writing instrument close by to make notes for when you wake up. This will be your dream notebook.

Get comfortable in a quiet setting with no distractions, preferably *just before* going to sleep. A warm bath beforehand may be helpful.

Slowly and deeply breathe in and out for about 3-4 breaths, close your eyes, and relax.

Review your day, starting from the beginning. Remember everything of importance that happened that day, whether you liked it or not. Remember. Focus. Release.

Next say aloud, **"I am going to have one dream tonight and I will become aware *as I'm dreaming it.*"** Breathe. Relax. Repeat that phrase 4-5 times. Breathe. Relax.

Then go to sleep.

If you need to keep rhythmically breathing and relaxing for a while to help you go to sleep, please do so.

As you become aware you are lucid while dreaming, pay close attention. Look at your hand. Look around. Do items shift as you look around? Is anything happening? Are any persons there with you? What are your surroundings? Notice everything.

When you are done with the lucid dream, wake up and write down that dream in your dream notebook. Even if it is just a few words. An image. A feeling.

When you wake up again (either in the middle of the night or in the morning), write down any other dreams you can remember in your dream note-book. Even if it is just a few words. An image. A feeling.

Advanced – Problem solving while lucid dreaming—Nights 7, 8, 9 and so on:

Keep a special notepad with a writing instrument close by to make notes for when you wake up. This will be your dream notebook.

Get comfortable in a quiet setting with no distractions, preferably just before going to sleep. A warm bath beforehand or some gentle stretching may be helpful.

Slowly and deeply breathe in and out for about 3-4 breaths, close your eyes, and relax.

Review your day starting from the beginning. Remember everything of importance that happened that day, whether you liked it or not. Remember. Focus. Release.

Now think of a problem you would like to resolve.

Then say aloud, **"Tonight I am going to work on a problem while I am lucidly dreaming. I am going to have one dream tonight and I will be aware as I'm dreaming it. I WILL work through my problem *in my lucid dream state."*** Breathe. Relax. Repeat that phrase 4-5 times. Breathe. Relax.

Then go to sleep.

If you need to keep rhythmically breathing and relaxing for a while to help you go to sleep, please do so.

When you become aware you are lucid while dreaming, pay close attention. Look at your hand. Look around. Do items shift as you look around? Is anything happening? Are any persons there with you? What are your surroundings? Notice everything.

Remember your decision to work on a problem while dreaming and then do so. If you need help to work on your problem, you can call on anyone or anything to help you. [In my first few lucid dreams doing problem solving, I called on: *1) the Marines, 2) Superman, 3) Jesus , 4) an elevator technician.*]

When you are finished with the lucid dream, wake up and write down that dream in your dream notebook. Even if it is just a few words. An image. A feeling. When you wake up again (either in the middle of the night or in the morning), write down any other dreams you can remember in your dream notebook. Even if it is just a few words. An image. A feeling.

Continue to practice.

***

RITUAL GROUP MEDITATION EXERCISE TRAVELING IN YOUR ETHERIC BODY TO MT. SHASTA – EXERCISE #4

This is the time to practice attending the ritual group meditation as you did at the end of Class #1. Although you may want to skip this exercise, I encourage you to repeat it often as it will stimulate your growth.

Tape recorder or cellphone: You can use a tape recorder or a cellphone to make a recording of the original exercise to or go to YouTube to listen to the descriptions.

Notebook: Journal your experiences when finished.

***

If you have questions or concerns, you may send me an email at *thyme.lauren@gmail.com.*

***

At this point you may "take down" —remove—your Lemurian 6-pointed star formation. As you do so, pay attention to discerning an energy shift. Can you feel the difference?

Notebook: Write down any experiences, insights and transformations you had. Write down your experiences with the Lemurian Star.

[1] Carl Calleman, *The Nine Waves of Creation*, p. 22
2 Carl Calleman, *The Nine Waves of Creation,* p. 267
3 Carl Calleman, *The Nine Waves of Creation,* p. 263

LIVING IN THE NEW LEMURIA:

EXERCISES, PRACTICES, AND TECHNIQUES

Class #8
Being Psychic & Telepathic, Listening with Compassion

***

LEMURIAN STAR – MERKABA – SACRED GEOMETRY

Set up your Lemurian 6-pointed star before you begin your class. Part of what you are learning is to pay close attention to energy and energy shifts. Using the 6-pointed Lemurian Star helps to increase and improve energy when you do the exercises within the Star.

***

CHALLENGES

> Lauren's Law #32: "Challenges are required, like rainwater, in order to learn and grow."

Challenges are here to help us grow. Even the worst, most difficult challenges are gifts for your soul to gain great wisdom and knowledge. Earth is one of the most difficult 3rd dimension planets to come to. The learning may be tough, yet the learning is permanent.

A warrior seeks out difficult training to become the best.

"A spiritual warrior goes to the toughest boot camp she can find." — Dr. Schultz Our soul is here to learn, not receive handouts or test scores ahead of time. Spiritual learning is transformative, potent 9th wave energy which is meant to heal lifetimes and our planet.

Dr. Michael Newton, author of *Journey of Souls: Case Studies of Life between Lives,* was a spiritual counselor to 10,000 people and studied them in extensive investigations. According to Dr. Newton's studies, each soul decides in the life between lives what we want to do, learn and heal in each incarnation.

With a myriad of choices, our Higher Self with our Spiritual Guides create an astrology chart. A chart which indicates a lot of challenges is actually more beneficial than one with too few.

Hermann Hesse said in Siddhartha, "Whether you and I and a few others will renew the world someday remains to be seen… within ourselves we must renew it each day."

Many of us who chose to be here on Earth at this challenging time are clear about what we are here to do:

1. Be of service

2. Be strong and resilient

3. Observe the challenges of Earth and ask how we can help

4. Be spiritual, peaceful, kind, and compassionate

5. Practice higher knowledge

6. Heal our own lifetimes and karma

QUESTIONS FROM THE HIGHER SELF - EXERCISE #24

Get out your notebook. Take off your logical mind and set it aside. Relax yourself and breathe. Go up to your Higher Self and answer these questions from that perspective.

Notebook: Answer the following questions

1. What am I here to heal in myself?

2. What karma, decisions and problems from past lives am I here to heal?

3. Who do I know on this planet who is here to challenge me?

4. Who do I know who is here to love and support me?

5. What are my skills and talents that I brought with me?

6. Why do I have the problems, challenges and difficulties that confront me?

7. What do I most need to learn and practice?

8. What am I most impatient with?

9. Why did I choose the family of origin that I have? Parents? Siblings?

10. Why did I choose this body?

11. Why did I choose my partner? (If there is more than one, name each and answer the question).

12. What do I most yearn for?

13. What did I do or not do in past lives that I want to make up for in this life? Who did I hurt?

14. Am I willing to forgive myself for perpetuating these wrong-doings?

Notebook: What stood out for you in this exercise? Were there any surprises? Did it clarify the mission you set up for yourself in this lifetime? Any other comments, thoughts or feelings when doing this exercise?

***

PAYING ATTENTION and BECOMING MORE PSYCHIC

We can choose to live, work, think and feel in accordance with the 9th wave of creation, the final step in human evolution of unity, harmony, and conscious co-creation. The 9th wave is powerfully connected to our extra senses. What if everyone were psychic?

Lauren's Law #25: "Everyone is psychic."

All of us are psychic. That ability, known as discernment, is found within our physical body, linked to our Higher Selves and to the Divine also known as Creator Source.

We discern through 5 extra senses, known as extrasensory perception, which is similar to our five physical senses of seeing, hearing, feeling, smelling and tasting. These abilities are connected to Creator Source through which we can pick up messages from the Divine and learn about our part of the Divine Plan. These abilities help us to become more connected to each other and our planet which includes plants, animals, land, water, and air as well as the Devas, Angelic Beings who govern those. Deva is a Sanskrit word which translates to heavenly, divine, terrestrial beings of high excellence, exalted, shining ones. When exercising ESP, one can hear, see and feel Devas.

The 5 extra senses are clairvoyance which is seeing, clairaudience hearing, clairsentience feeling, clairalience smelling, and clairgustance tasting. These are included in many of our exercises which encourages us to see, hear, feel, smell and taste in a more focused octave of skill. The extra senses work on a higher level, resonance or dimension, which is like having an extra and higher set of eyes, ears and so on, which continually builds our discernment muscles.

Lauren's Law #19: "There is no such thing as a lie, not even a 'little white lie'" because humans are all psychic. This includes telling outright falsehoods as well as failing to tell the truth. Lies cannot and do not exist. Everyone intuits another's emotions and intentions and behaves according to that intuition, even if the intuition is unconscious. Attempting to lie (or failing to tell the truth) will create problems for everyone, especially oneself. Many of today's world problems are based on attempts to lie. Many movies are based on the interaction around a falsehood. That kind of movie plot can't exist without an attempt to conceal, hide, avoid, or run from the truth; the movie would be over in a matter of minutes had the truth been told at the beginning.

Lauren's Law #18: "Tell the truth......as fast as you can – with kindness and gentleness." This may not mean immediately. Sometimes appropriate timing is involved. Truth opens up avenues of opportunities and possibilities that may not have been exposed before.

Lies create barriers and deterioration between individuals and groups which continue to grow until the truth is revealed by the person(s) who lied. Amends may be necessary in order to heal damaged trust and broken relationships.

THREE SIMPLE STEPS TO BECOMING MORE PSYCHIC
EXERCISE #25

For the next week pay attention using the 3 instructions below:

1. **Pay attention to each message you receive.** Hear (clairaudient), feel (clairsentient), see (clairvoyant), smell, or taste. The message can come from your Higher Self, the Divine Mind or from something outside yourself – such as a movie, video, internet, billboard, book, words from another person, a Guide or Deva, etc.

2. **Trust the message you get.** The logical mind may doubt, discuss, hesitate, distrust, dismiss, discourage, or ignore the message. The logical mind is not helpful in this regard.

3. If part of the message requires action, be sure to **take that action.**

[Years ago, I wanted to sell my permaculture farm, but wasn't able to do so and gave up. A year later I got a message from the Elders: "Sell your farm NOW!" I sent out 50 emails to anyone who might have been interested. One of the 50 people sent a message to one of their customers who wanted to buy an organic farm. The buyers arrived the next day with a full price offer and the sale was completed without a hitch.]

Notebook: Write down your experiences of becoming more psychic while using the 3 instructions above.

***

TELEPATHY – EXERCISE #26

This exercise requires 2 people. Choose a partner, someone whom you like and trust.

Steps: Set up an appointment for a definite time every day, at least once per day, for 7 days in a row.

Remember the time difference if you live far apart. Make sure that both of you will be awake at that time.

Set an alarm. At the scheduled time, think of that person by name, face, energy, scent or voice. Focus for at least 30 seconds. At the same time, that person will be thinking of you.

Notebook: Write down any impression you receive, no matter how slight or fleeting, including what you felt, saw, heard, smelled or tasted.

Contact that person by phone or email immediately and share your impressions.

If neither of you receive anything, don't worry. Practicing will strengthen the abilities of each of you. Keep repeating daily.

Notebook: If you think of that person at a different time than arranged, including nighttime or upon awakening during the night or morning, get out your notebook and write down any impression you received, no matter how slight or fleeting, including what you felt, saw, heard, smelled or tasted.

Contact your person by phone or email as soon as possible after writing in your notebook and share your impressions.

Why is this important in your training? Lemurians were highly telepathic and paid close attention to "messages" they received. Doing this exercise frequently will strengthen your bond with the person you chose and can activate higher emotions such as bliss, forgiveness, courage, and enlightenment.

Notebook: Write about your experiences with the other person. Are you a better sender or receiver?

ACTIVE LISTENING with COMPASSION - EXERCISE #27

Active listening with compassion is an Elder virtue attached to Gold Light Wisdom.

Active listening with compassion is helpful in dealing with another person's disharmonious emotions and difficulties.

Active listening with compassion is particularly valuable for us in these classes as we deepen our senses of empathy, compassion and telepathy.

Steps: Here are some suggestions on how to actively listen with compassion:

> Avoid giving advice unless the speaker asks it. Then keep it short and sweet.
> Resist the temptation to fix. Fixing subtly implies the speaker is incapable of self-help.
> Nod your head.
> Avoid interrupting.
> Ask pertinent questions.
> Rather than assume something from the other person, clarify, ask questions, restate – "Is that correct?"

You can ask:

> "Is there anything else you would like to say or want me to know?"

"Is there anything I can do to help?"

"I'm sorry you're going through …."

Wait until the speaker is completely finished to begin your own story.

If you listen well enough without advising, interrupting, or lecturing, the speaker will find his or her own path to their own truth and conclusions, often leading to relief and a movement towards a more harmonious emotion and a diminishing of discomfort. If actions or resolutions are needed, the speaker will find those through his or her own process, supported by compassionate, active listening. Every person has the means to find his or her own truth, especially with the support of compassionate listening.

Notebook: At least once a day practice active listening with compassion and write down your experiences.

***

RITUAL GROUP MEDITATION EXERCISE TRAVELING IN YOUR ETHERIC BODY TO MT. SHASTA - EXERCISE #4

This is the time to practice attending the ritual group meditation as you did at the end of Class #1. I encourage you to repeat it often as it will stimulate your growth.

Tape recorder or cellphone: You can use a tape recorder or a cellphone to make a recording of the original exercise to or go to YouTube to listen to the descriptions.

Notebook: Journal your experiences when finished.

***

If you have questions or concerns, you may send me an email at *thyme.lauren@gmail.com.*

∗∗∗

At this point you may "take down"—remove—your Lemurian 6-pointed star formation. As you do so, pay attention to discerning an energy shift. Can you feel the difference?

Notebook: Write down any experiences, insights and transformations you had in this class. Write down your experiences with the Lemurian Star.

Journey of Souls: Case Studies of Life between Lives, Dr. Michael Newton © 1994
The Nine Waves of Creation, Dr. Carl Calleman © 2016
Siddhartha, Hermann Hesse © 1981

LIVING IN THE NEW LEMURIA:

EXERCISES, PRACTICES, AND TECHNIQUES

Class #9
Manifesting, Astrology, Karma/Evolution, Voice Fighting

***

LEMURIAN STAR – MERKABA – SACRED GEOMETRY

You will do your next exercises sitting inside your Lemurian Star formation. Please seat yourself within the Lemurian star and await whatever miracles may occur. The ancient Lemurians worked extensively with crystals. You may wish to place crystals inside your Lemurian star.

***

MANIFESTING MIRACLES EXERCISE - #28

Miracles include physical objects, people, abilities, training, insights and help that you either asked for—or **didn't** ask for. Miracles can include anything. Miracles are not necessarily gradations of manifestation. To us humans, some miracles seem trivial to manifest, while others may seem huge. In the Universe there are no small nor large miracles—only miracles.

Notebook: Get out your notebook. Write down the following instructions:

1. *Every* time you manifest ANYTHING you are pleased to receive, whether or not you consciously requested it, write it down in your notebook, including what showed up and the date.

2. If there was a price you paid for the manifestation, note that as well, especially if the price is a bargain!

3. If you intuited or got a message that your manifestation was waiting for you at a specific place or time and you found it was true, write that down.

4. On your monthly spread sheet while planning for future income and bill paying, include 2 new categories for unexpected income – *Miracles* and *Miscellaneous.*

5. Thank Creator Source for each miracle. Gratitude perpetuates more miracles and manifestations.

[I thank Creator Source for parking spaces and thank my plants as an envoy of Creator Source when I pick vegetables or herbs from the garden.]

Lauren's Law #20: "Everything is connected to everything as though by an immense Spider Web of Life."

You are always connected to *everything* in the Universe. Through this exercise you are learning to pay attention to your miraculous manifestations. Your manifestation muscles will get stronger each time.

Manifesting using this technique makes your life easier and requires minimal effort. You will begin to manifest other miracles (things you did and didn't ask for) as well.

Miracles are connected to conscious co-creation. You work as a partner with Creator Source in the 9th wave. All you need to do is to pay attention to the miracles that manifest from Creator Source and accept those graciously. You can also practice manifesting by attaching sticky notes of requests around your home or office and write them in your notebook to remind yourself.

PRIMING THE PUMP

One important aspect of receiving miracles from Creator Source is what I call "priming the pump." The meaning of this phrase is to encourage the growth or action of something, as in "Marjorie tried to prime the pump by offering some new issues for discussion." In the late 1800's this expression originally was used for pouring liquid into a pump to expel the air and make it work. In the 1930's, it was applied to government efforts to stimulate the economy and applied to other undertakings as well."—Wikipedia, "priming the pump"

When I say "prime the pump" I mean to stimulate or support the growth of something, including miracles, through positive action.

Affirmation exercises like the ones taught in this course are excellent. Yet one must take "realistic" steps, certain measures, in order to prime the pump. In other words, you do your part so that Creator Source can make miracles happen for you.

When I was in my early 30's, I had an affirmations teacher named Richard whom I worked with every week. Richard seemed excellent – for a time. At one point he lost money and clients. He was on the verge of being evicted from his apartment, while he didn't have enough money for utilities and food. He wrote hundreds of affirmations and hung them up all over his apartment. He didn't take any other steps though, like getting a regular job or trying to find clients or applying for food stamps. He just sat in his apartment and waited for his affirmations to come to fruition.

I asked him why he wasn't taking action to help himself. "Don't you have to do something? Like prime the pump?" I asked him.

Richard merely pointed at his affirmations posted everywhere. He didn't take any other action. Eventually he was evicted, had to move out and became homeless at that point. I stopped seeing him as my teacher as I felt he was lacking an important component of affirmations—namely taking important action to prime the pump.

Here's a joke – with meaning:

> Once there was a man named John who lived in the flood region of the Midwest with his family in a 2-story house.
>
> One summer an intense storm came, and flood waters started to rise around his house.
> John sent his wife and kids away to safety, while he stayed. "God will save me," he told them.
>
> The water rose higher.
> A neighbor with a boat motored by and he waved the neighbor away. "God will save me."
>
> The water rose higher still.
> Then a Coast Guard helicopter flew overhead and lowered a ladder for John. He waved the helicopter away. "It's okay," he yelled to them. "God will save me." The helicopter flew away.

The water rose higher until John climbed to the roof of his house, while the murky water lapped at his feet.

A county motorboat came by, loaded with people. John waved that boat away too. "I'll wait here. God will save me. Thanks anyway."

The water rose over his roof and John drowned.
When John got to the pearly gates of heaven, he was furious. He asked St. Peter why God didn't save him from the flood.

St. Peter shrugged his shoulders. "God sent you two boats and a helicopter!"

In the Holy Bible it is written "Ask and ye shall receive." Matthew Chapter 7, Verse 7.

"Be thankful and accept every miracle that shows up!" Lauren O. Thyme, *Living in the New Lemuria*

Often you may find that miracles and manifestations have a calendar of their own.

ASTROLOGY

Lauren's Law #13: "The Universe is all about timing. So is everything in your life."

One insufficiently understood, even disparaged, component of this 3-dimensional world is we are living in an interactive, constantly changing and evolving energetic solar system as part of the Universe. Many well-respected scientists and knowledgeable people have also been astrologers such as Hippocrates, Galileo, Johannes Kepler, Isaac Newton and Dr. Carl Jung. The sign a planet goes through, the kinds of interactions planets have with each other in real time, and how they affect our personal astrology charts and influence physical events are components of astrology.

This was especially true of Covid-19 in 2020, influencing elections, stimulating social unrest, wars, economics, collective spiritual movements, changes in your personal life, and so forth. While you cannot change the planets and their actions, you can practice the exercises taught in these classes to ameliorate the effects. You can also practice remembering that you are in the 9th wave of creation as clarified by the Mayan calendar. The universal energy and purpose of the evolving Universe via the 9th wave is encouraging you and all of us to focus on unity, harmony and conscious co-creation.

"I believe that the entire Universe is in a giant conspiracy for our ultimate well-being, if we can listen to its promptings."[1]—David Pond, astrologer

PAST LIVES, KARMA and EVOLUTION

All past lives are running in present time, so the phrase "*past lives*" is an imprecise term. A person can change a past life by changing her present life. A person can also change her present life by changing her past life. A person can change a past life error by forgiving that past life self.

Lauren's Law #16: "Instant Karma – Karma can be quick depending on your awareness, for the purpose of instant learning. The more you learn, the more aware you become, the faster Karma works. It is a self-reinforcing loop."

Saturn, Lord of Karma, is considered the planet of rules, regulations, and responsibilities. It is important to note, however, that karma is not about punishment, rather we can look at it as fuel for the growth of our soul. Karma brings to us whatever our soul needs to ascend and evolve higher. Karma brings to us whatever is going to help us navigate the path of our higher selves. As the Lord of Karma, we can view Saturn as a strict teacher. The work it presents to us is challenging, hard, and can seem almost impossible, but once we start to get the hang of it, we can grow, prosper, and become much wiser than before. Saturn, Jupiter, and Pluto have traveled together in Capricorn since December 2019, stimulating the effects we have experienced in 2020.

Lauren's Law #17: "Grace trumps Karma."

BLUEPRINT

The blueprint of your life, what your soul came in to do, is reflected in your birth chart including talents, skills, personality, relationships, challenges, health, and difficulties.

As an astrologer I believe there is no such thing as free will. Your life was defined by your soul before you were conceived in the life between lives. During your entire life you work within those parameters. The movements of planets, known as transits, show how your life will be from year to year including short periods and long periods of time. Your progressed chart shows your development through your life, still within a pre-determined framework of what you chose.

In the same way, the transits of the planets affect Earth which then affect us. We planned to show up at a particular place and time, with whatever would be happening, for our learning, growth and evolution.

Our past lives operate in the same way, attuned to the social, economic and spiritual milieu of the planet, working within the 9 waves of creation, according to the Mayan calendar.

You can hire a reputable astrologer or study astrology yourself to learn more. While the forces behind astrology are powerful, astrology is merely an instrument which discloses tendencies, trends and predispositions. I'm not talking about the popular horoscope section you can read in a newspaper or magazine. I am a professionally trained astrologer with 40 years of experience and understand the intricacies of an astrological chart. Charts are amazingly complex, while the interpretation of them takes years of practice and excellent intuition. Before computers, it took me 4 hours to "erect" a birth chart.

Lauren's Law #21: "Everything is perfect, no matter what it looks like, for the purpose of growing, learning and evolving."

Since astrology contains the blueprint which shows how each of us fits into the Divine Plan, the more you know yourself, the better you can accept, surrender, and be grateful.

There is no such thing as free will. We are part of a Divine Plan. However, we can decide how to react to something. Your astrology chart, the blueprint of your life, shows you what you have come here to work with including skills, desires, opportunities, challenges, and difficulties. God is in charge.

> "You will have a really clear idea of who you are, what you want, where you are going, and how to get there."[2]
> —Pam Gregory, astrologer at www.thenextstep.uk.com

Energy from planets, sun, moon and asteroids show tendencies and proclivities that take years of practice to deduce, like a modern-day Sherlock Holmes. Maurice Fernandez is one of those brilliant and intuitive astrologers. He practices evolutionary astrology, a holistic approach to the practice of astrology and the art of living.

Maurice Fernandez, David Pond, Pam Gregory, Rob Hand (from Astrodienst), and other professional astrologers worldwide check the movements of planets daily. These movements correlate precisely, often to the day, with what is happening on the planet. Astrologers were studying the astrological implications of 2020 for years. Based on the planets and signs involved,

- they anticipated certain scenarios, all of which transpired:

- the emergence of a pandemic;

- the economic downturns of countries around the planet;

- civil unrest, demonstrations, looting and murder.

Maurice Fernandez's website contains 4 lengthy YouTube videos explaining in fascinating detail in plain English what has been going on astrologically in 2020 and how it affects all of us.

Lauren's Law #22: "Everything is perfect, no matter whether it changes or not."

In his weekly forecast for Dec. 7-13, 2020, David Pond stated: "We are nearing the end of the daunting Jupiter/Saturn/Pluto conjunction in Capricorn that has defined and shaped 2020. Not this week, but the week following, Saturn and Jupiter will both be moving into forward thinking Aquarius, ending the Capricorn gridlock, which has been like the movie, 'Groundhog Day' in confronting us with the same challenges, day after day. So, keep heart, the end of this heavy energy is close upon us. Spirits can get lifted this week with the Sun in optimistic Sagittarius supported by Mars, the planet of action, in Aries. This activates personal confidence in your ability to move forward."[1]

Because I am considered a "Plutonian,"[3] one of my most valued books is *Healing Pluto Problems* written by Donna Cunningham, an astrologer and trained psychologist. Although downsized by astronomers to a large asteroid, Pluto is a transformational and challenging planet for individuals and is one of the major planets affecting us in 2020. Like Carl Jung, Donna employed psychology and counseling coupled with astrology to help thousands of people during her life.

Confusion swirls around Pluto. Dr. Mark Littmann, University of Tennessee-Knoxville astronomy and journalism professor, as well as author of an award-winning book on the solar system, says, "Pluto is too large to be an asteroid because it has about three times more mass than all the asteroids in the solar system put together... Secondly, he says, Pluto is in the wrong place to be an asteroid. The vast majority of asteroids orbit the Sun between Mars and Jupiter."[4]

Yet this small planetoid which rules power, nuclear energy and volcanos is partly responsible for the abrupt transformation of our planet in 2020. Its satellites are highly unusual in our solar system. "Pluto, the dwarf planet that was once considered the ninth planet, has a growing entourage of satellites. The tiny world has five moons of varying size in orbit around it that tumble and dance in a strange and chaotic pattern...The way I would describe this system is not just *chaos, but pandemonium,* Mark Showalter, a co-investigator on the New Horizons mission, said at a press conference last November."[5] Pluto and its satellites can be studied to understand the chaotic transformations that Pluto elicits.

I believe that Pluto is a star gate from the Milky Way Galaxy into our solar system. Lemurians apparently traveled from other galaxies through the Pluto stargate, on to Venus and eventually to Earth.

Pluto will be remembered and recorded in the annals of astrology, as well as in the Akashic Records, as a major participant of the ordeals Earth citizens faced in 2020.

To get your free natal chart interpretation, please email thyme.lauren@gmail.com

To get your free personal daily forecast, and to cast your own chart, sign up at Astrodienst. https://www.astro.com

THE BATTLE OF BELIEFS REVISITED

Speaking of 2020, the battle of beliefs became stronger and more polarized in 2020.

"As an astrologer, I am blessed with clients from all walks of life, religions and political views—astrology encompassing all these orientations and favoring none. Listening to my clients …has given me insights into the polarization occurring in our country, with nearly as many people deeply disappointed in the outcome of the election as those who are relieved and uplifted. It is particularly sad… [when] family members and friends can no longer communicate because of polarized beliefs."
—David Pond, astrologer

Lauren's Law #1: "We each live in our own separate Universe. Everything in that Universe is true and correct for that Universe. There is no truth with a capital T, no reality with a capital R."

You may flinch when listening to someone you don't agree with expound on his or her beliefs *as if it is the paramount and only Truth available.* Even scientific truths have become polarized along with spiritual, metaphysical and new age truths, each having its own belief systems and even sub-belief systems. This includes medical science with traditional, allopathic medicine as divergent from holistic, homeopathic, non-traditional, and functional medicine.

The Lemurian Elders warn of frozen belief systems. "When searching for meaning, a danger lies in finding a piece of knowledge, then freezing it into a selective meaning of a belief or ideology."—*The Lemurian Way*, pg. 104

One can know one's own experiences, using discernment and resonance, yet many people rely on news, the internet, or repeating what someone else reports.

Everyone lives in their own personal reality.

[I had a vision back in 1997 when discussing President Clinton with Donna, my dear friend, at dinner while trying to figure out if the President was lying. Clinton hadn't yet admitted to his affair with Monica Lewinsky.

Suddenly the ceiling of the restaurant blew away and I found myself floating in the blackness of space. All around her were tiny images looking like miniature cornucopias. She was informed that each cornucopia was a separate Universe representing one person on earth. "We each live in our own separate Universe," the Elders explained to her. "Everything in that Universe is true and correct for that Universe. There is no truth with a capital T, no reality with a capital R."

Then I returned to normal life in the restaurant with my friend Donna, eventually incorporating my vision into Lauren's Laws.]

One's personal experience through discernment, using one's 5 senses and 5 extra senses, is a reliable way to find your own truth.

Other information is difficult to know absolutely without having unwavering faith in a source outside yourself. In the current political, religious and scientific climates, believing can often be difficult.

Remember, the 2nd step to becoming more psychic is—*trust your own answers*—as if your life depends on those answers. It does.

Relief usually follows trusting your own answer. You can trust the feeling of relief too. It is a guidepost to stay aware of.

A personal reality, which you can discern in your body, can include goosebumps (I call them truth bumps), especially full body goosebumps, hair standing on end, crying, shivering, sensations in various chakras, a feeling in the pit of your stomach, and kriyas. "Movements in Kundalini yoga are referred to as kriyas [sudden releases of energy] and they're meant to help release the *kundalini* energy, which is said to lay coiled at the bottom of the spine, lying dormant, until the energy is set free."[6] Sometimes kriyas happen spontaneously with spiritual exercises, meditations, and rebirthing also known as conscious breathing.

How to state your personal BELIEF without polarization, while being absolutely clear:

> I believe…
> I think…
> It's my opinion that…
>
> rather than lecture, harangue or speak as if one's belief is the absolute Truth. That kind of behavior only serves to separate rather than unify, leading to a battle of beliefs.

Being overpowered by someone's belief feels inharmonious and jarring. The same is true of trying to convince someone of your belief. It might be outside their understanding or experience and can feel like an assault on their consciousness. At that point, most people rebel.

I have a favorite mantra: "I don't know" which is helpful while stating your own personal truth and avoiding arguments.

You can experiment to see what your truth feels like in your own separate universe using discernment and noticing what resonates. Your body and feelings are major players in this process, experiencing goose flesh, crying, shivers, gut feelings, kriyas, plus sensations in the heart and other chakras.

Lauren's Law #27: "The mind is not my friend."

One cannot use the logical mind for discernment as belief systems and traditional thought are already embedded and entrenched in the mind, part of the 6th, 7th, and 8th waves of the Mayan calendar.

VOICE FIGHTING… AGAIN – EXERCISE #29

The imbedded Voice can play a game of denigrating and judging another person.

Lauren's Law #10: "When a difficult person arrives in your life, love that person, forgive and be grateful. The Universe has sent that person to you as a gift for your learning."

Lauren's Law #23: "Forgiveness is selfish – for your own peace, happiness and well-being."

Lauren's Law #14: "There is no one to blame." It's a no-fault unverse.

Voice Game #7: Low esteem of others; blame, dislike, hate and judgments. "That person made me..."

Your constructive responses can be:

> Voice, I forgive...(name the person)*
> Voice, I am not a victim.
> Voice, I don't have to complain, whine or protest.
> Voice, it's not their fault.
> Voice, that person is not a happy camper.
> Voice, no one can make me do something I don't want to do.
> Voice, I choose what I want and don't want.
> Voice, if I listen to you, I will dislike other people and create separation and loneliness.
> Voice, I'm ignoring you now.
> Voice, go away! Leave me alone! Shut up!

* *For more information you can read and practice* **Forgiveness equals Fortune** *by Liah Holtzman and Lauren O. Thyme — available on Amazon.*

Homework: Create a seventh 3" x 5" card with Game #7 on it along with the constructive responses.

Keep that card with you for those occasions when the Voice plays its game with you as you do with the other cards.

***

RITUAL GROUP MEDITATION EXERCISE TRAVELING IN YOUR ETHERIC BODY TO MT. SHASTA – EXERCISE #4

This is the time to practice attending the ritual group meditation as you did at the end of Class #1. Although you may want to skip this exercise, I encourage you to repeat it often as it will stimulate your growth.

Tape recorder or cellphone: You can use a tape recorder or a cellphone to make a recording of the original exercise to or go to YouTube to listen to the descriptions.

***

If you have questions or concerns, you may send me an email at *thyme.lauren@gmail.com.*

***

At this point you may "take down"—remove—your Lemurian 6-pointed star formation. As you do so, pay attention to discerning an energy shift. Can you feel the difference?

Notebook: Write down experiences, insights and transformations you had in this class. Write down your experiences with the Lemurian Star.

---

[1] David Pond.com
[2] Pam Gregory, www.thenextstep.uk.com
[3] *Healing Pluto Problems*, Donna Cunningham

[4] The Debate: Is Pluto A Planet, Asteroid Or Comet? News (utk.edu)

[5] Pluto's Moons | Five Satellites of Pluto, Space.com

[6] Understanding Kriyas and Kundalini, (yogapedia.com)

Maurice Fernandez.com, astrologer

Journey of Souls, The Life Between Lives, Dr. Michael Newton

Forgiveness equals Fortune, Liah Holtzman and Lauren O. Thyme

LIVING IN THE NEW LEMURIA:

EXERCISES, PRACTICES, AND TECHNIQUES

Class #10
Relationships, Evolution of Consciousness, Blame, Cutting Cords

**

LEMURIAN STAR – MERKABA – SACRED GEOMETRY

Set up this star before your class. Please seat yourself within the gold star. Feel the energy inside. Ancient Lemurians used crystals extensively. Please feel free to add crystals to your Lemurian Star formation.

**

You may find it helpful to remind yourself that the evolution of our planet is fluid and dynamic, as connected to the Divine Plan. We humans may only get glimpses of that Plan and our place in it, yet we are connected to all 9 waves of creation which are in motion into infinity.

The 6th wave wave (3115 BCE) contains duality and the idea of *us versus them,* good versus evil, including nationalism, ideologies and religions. Evil does not exist except within the 6th wave hologram. Consequently, those who have acted in evil ways, like Adolph Hitler or Saddam Hussein, teach us about acceptance and forgiveness.

The 7th wave (1755 CE) activated the rational, logical mind, yet separate from Creator Source. The 8th wave (1999 CE) incorporates our right brain, intuitive, feminine side and technology, especially computers and the internet, while focusing on the Eastern half of our planet.

The 9th and final wave (2011) triggers unity, harmony and conscious co-creation with each other and Creator Source. Awareness, and practice is necessary to cement and anchor those attributes into our planetary consciousness. Although 6th wave consciousness is about "us versus them," there is really only "us" as we are now morphing into the 9th wave. We can be part of the solution rather than the problem, while there's no one to blame.

Ken Wilber, in his innovative book *Up from Eden,* explains the evolution of consciousness moving from undifferentiated us, to us versus them, and finally to us in a transpersonal level of evolution and consciousness. See below…

Pre-personal stages

Uroboric – indistinguishable connection; from 3 million to 200,000 years ago

Typhonic – dragons, monsters, gods; from 200,000 to 10,000 BCE

Mythic – heroes; began 11,000 BCE; development of farming consciousness and mythic membership; an extended sense of time developed while full-fledged language appeared.

Personal – Us versus Them

Mental/Egoic   a new stage of "Solar Ego" consciousness emerged
in 2500 BCE: Rugged individualism, Psychic

Transpersonal – Us   respecting each other as sovereign "I / Thou" – 9th wave

Spiritual   heart centered rather than mind centered
Void 1   containing everything and nothing
Void 2   containing everything and nothing

Lauren's Law #1: "We each live in our own separate Universe"
which is nearing 8 billion Universes.

***

WHAT IF THERE IS NO ONE TO BLAME FOR OUR PROBLEMS?

first published Galde Press, June 21, 2012; excerpt from *Cosmic Grandma Wisdom*
© 2017 Lauren O. Thyme

"I notice problems here on our planet. We may derive comfort from blaming someone or something for those problems. But does blaming someone else solve those problems?

Adult Children of Alcoholics has a saying: 'When I point a finger at someone, there are 3 fingers pointing back at me.'

Blame is like a MONSTER.

'He who fights with monsters should be careful lest he thereby become a monster. And if thou gaze long into an abyss, the abyss will also gaze into thee.'
—Friedrich Nietzsche, *Of Good and Evil*

I believe no one is to blame for those problems. Not you. Not me. Not the Illuminati or the Bankers or Politicians or some Other Religion or Draconians or God.

'Everything is perfect, no matter what it looks like, for the purpose of growth, learning and evolution,' say my Council of Elders. It has been my mantra for thirty years.

As time went by, we human beings learned. We learned religion. We learned building. We learned growing food. We learned technology. Most of us believed that the planet belonged to us exclusively. That we were the sovereign masters over all we surveyed. We wanted to control nature and each other. We wanted to invent things. We wanted energy to further improve our lifestyles. We wanted money to do things and buy things and visit places far away.

All of us want more than we have, for ourselves, our family, and others. There is no fault in any of those wants. We are like eager children, ready to head over the horizon to the next frontier, the next tomorrow, often without realizing the costs.

Now we see that all our wanting and learning has brought us to where we are now. Not all of it is bad. We didn't mean to hurt each other or the planet or animals or nature. We got ahead of ourselves. Our consciousness didn't keep up with advanced technology, including weaponry. But there's no one to blame for it.

Many people are now awakening. They look around and are aghast. 'It must have been someone OUT THERE who did this.'

We weren't paying attention. We are now. Now we are learning and growing. The very problems that upset us—are the impetus to compel us to new learning.

I have spent many nights lying in bed, practicing forgiveness, being grateful to everyone, especially those whom I might otherwise want to blame. Blame doesn't make me feel better. Blame doesn't solve problems either.

Now it's time for cooperation. The ten trillion cells in each of our bodies know how to cooperate and work together. We can too.

I find that gratitude especially brings me to peace and happiness. I'm not saying it's easy. With repetition, the forgiveness, love and gratitude towards others shifts my attitudes, my life, even my physical body.

Perhaps this seems counter-intuitive to you. All I know is when I removes blame and finger-pointing from the equation, the equation begins to shift. Subtly at first, then stronger and stronger.

Blame is the old paradigm of the 6th wave and it's time for the new 9th wave of harmony, unity and Divine Connection.

Therefore, we can continue to bless those whom we might be tempted to blame for our problems. There is no *them*. There is only *us*."

We are connected to one another as one heart, one harmonious family as we strive for I - Thou relationships to people, animals, the planet and Creator Source.

"The notion of **I-Thou** was developed by the twentieth-century philosopher Martin Buber appeared in his famous work of the same name *I and Thou*. The term refers to the primacy of the direct or immediate encounter which occurs between a human person and another being. This other being might be another person, another living or inanimate thing, or even God, which is the Eternal Thou. Buber contrasted this more fundamental relation of I-Thou with the I-It relationship which refers to our experience of others in an *unenlightened, unaware* state of being."

—New World Encyclopedia

Lauren's Law #2: "Love is the building block of the universe, from which everything emanates." It's in you, around you, it **IS** you. If you cannot feel love right now, don't worry. It's still there.

***

RELATIONSHIPS - CUTTING CORDS USING GOLD LIGHT

During our long sojourn in the cosmos, particularly on three-dimensional Earth, souls become attached to various persons. Generally, the cords of attachments can become particularly onerous and act like a weight, like a ship with multiple anchors drowning itself in deep waters.

These attachments can be emotional, physical, sexual, romantic, financial, familial, or professional, or based on perceived obligations, responsibilities, and debts or any combination thereof.

None of these attachments are necessary, except for one—the Gold Light of Unconditional Love between your heart and another's. Any other bonds bog you down and endure into perpetuity, while you might helplessly return to similar persons and scenarios over and over, like a weary hamster on a wheel. Often uncut cords can lead you back to that same soul, creating difficulties and challenges throughout many lifetimes.

All that is needed is to break the attachment once and for all eternity and to cut those cords of connection.

Relationships are an important means through which humans learn, grow and evolve. Here's what I have noticed in life:

Lauren's Law #6: "I can unconditionally love someone, but do not have to go to dinner with him or her."

**Lauren's Law #7: "A relationship lasts as long as it lasts –
not one minute longer. And you'll know the moment
the relationship has ended."**

**Lauren's Law #8: "When a relationship comes to an end,
bless it and move on. There's no turning back once
that lesson is learned."**

**Lauren's Law #9: "Relationships are like buses - there's always the
next one to catch to take you to a new destination."**

**Lauren's Law #10: "When a difficult person arrives in your life,
love that person, forgive and be grateful. The universe has sent
that person to you as a gift for your learning."**

**Lauren's Law #15: "Ended relationships are not failures.
Once you are finished learning with a person, you are on
to the next (it might be yourself) for the purpose of
personal learning, growing and evolving."**

There are suitable, appropriate and simple ways to be in relationship as well as to end a relationship. One of the tools that can effectively help is called the Cutting of the Cords.

The cutting of the cords exercise can end all karmic attachments, taken one at a time. This exercise is to help you break free of unnecessary ties and lighten your load. Although it may seem counter-intuitive, this exercise is helpful, perhaps imperative, to disconnect ALL ties with EVERY person in your life and those from other lifetimes as well—except for the Gold Light between hearts. All you will ever need is Unconditional Love between your heart and that of another, as you break the karmic chain through cutting cords, then floating buoyant and free.

**The Elders: "In a relationship you utilize fight or flight.
The easiest way is to FLOAT."**

This exercise is particularly powerful to use with someone you have or had acute difficulties with—a partner or lover, friend, child, parent, other relative, neighbor, even a political figure—who, just thinking of this person, is cringe-worthy and upsetting.

Although this exercise may seem like a disguised form of forgiveness, it is a simple, straightforward practice, using Gold Light, Creator Source, and your own discernment.

Lauren's Law #3: "If it's easy, it's right."

You may generally find that this exercise can be done just once with most people, leading directly to completion, and then you feel relief. Other times with another individual, you don't feel "done" and you may desire to perform this exercise multiple times. You can use your discernment and pay attention to know when you are complete.

[I had one person with whom I had to do this exercise 3 times a day for 30 days until I felt finished!]

You may find it powerful to perform this exercise while taking a bath, the water acting as a spiritual medium for the healing. You can also include burning white or gold candles, surrounding yourself with crystals, a Merkaba or Lemurian Star, to aid in activation and accomplishing detachment easily. You can call on Angels, Devas, Guides, and other spiritual entities to be with you and support you while you do this process.

Before I share the exercise with you, I want to include one last word of advice. You may desire to detach from a specific person, yet that person's self may refuse to cooperate. This is an extremely uncommon occurrence, and it may not happen to you. However, in case you do come across this difficulty, I give you some suggestions on how to deal with that problem following steps 1 – 17 below.

CUTTING THE CORDS USING GOLD LIGHT – EXERCISE #30

Steps:

1. Be in a comfortable place where you will be undisturbed for at least 15 minutes. Turn off all electronic devices including your phone.

2. Take a few deep breaths and relax. Close your eyes. Create an imagined, impermeable Bubble of Golden Light surrounding you.

3. Imagine that Creator Source is floating above you in gold light. Gold Light was used by the Lemurians for all their sacred rituals and is the most powerful light in the Universe for transformation. You may have your own favorite name for this Higher Power—such as God, Goddess, Jesus, Shiva, Buddha, Allah, or the Divine. Whatever your chosen name is, focus on Creator Source right now.

4. Ask Creator Source to send Gold Light Blessings into your body through the top of your head. Feel the gold light warmth and peaceful flow as it enters your body. Allow it to radiate throughout your head, into your body, arms, legs and feet, then into the ground below you... Feel it also like a warm golden shower washing over the outside of your body, cleansing all impurities and removing stress.

5. Breathe again and feel the blessings you are receiving from Creator Source. You feel relaxed and receptive... Enlarge and expand that Gold Light Bubble around you to include a second person.

6. When you are ready, think of a person in your life from whom you would like to detach. You might choose to start with a person who is easy. You can increase the degree of difficulty as you become proficient with this exercise.

7. Bring that person into the expanded Gold Light Bubble which now surrounds both of you. Imagine that Creator Source is floating in gold light above that person.

8. Ask Creator Source to send Gold Light Blessings into that person's body through the top of his or her head. Sense and see the gold light warmth and peaceful flow as it enters the other person's body. Allow it to radiate throughout their head, into their body, arms, legs and feet, then into the ground below them.

9. Sense it like a warm golden shower washing over the outside of their body, cleansing all impurities and relaxing that person. Sense the blessings that person is receiving from Creator Source. Breathe.

   When you feel the time is right for both of you, while sensing relaxation in each of you, you will start the next procedure.

10. Imagine, see, feel, sense, and intuit the cords of attachment between you and the other person. The cords may appear as chains, rope, silken threads, branches of trees, roots of plants, or metallic bars. Notice where the cords attach from the other person to you. There may be a few cords, or dozens, hundreds or even thousands of cords. This is a good time to make it up as you remember that your imagination is part of your Higher Self's intelligence.

11. Pay close attention and notice where each cord is connected between the other person and you. For example, in a sexual cording, there may be cords between genitals, between other parts of the body like the mouth, eyes, ears, or any number of variations and combinations. Take your time to discern as many as you can. Make it up as needed.

12. Now imagine you have an instrument in your hand to appropriately cut those cords. If it is tree branches, you might want a chain saw or a tree saw. For silken threads, a small knife or scissors might do the trick. For metal bars you might want a metal cutter, a light saber or some other heavy-duty instrument. Make it up if you want to do so. It will be perfect for you. In fact, the more fabulous your imagination, the better it works!

13. Next imagine you have a container of Gold Light Healing Salve with you. Every time you cut a cord, apply some of the Gold Light Salve at the severed connection point on each of your bodies and notice it heal.

    For example, if you had a connection that you removed from the palm of your hand, apply the Salve to your palm. If it was connected to the other person at their forehead, apply the Salve to their forehead where you cut the connection. There may be numerous combinations. Pay attention to as many as you can.

Lauren's Law #24: "Pay attention as if your life depends on it. It does."

Make sure to apply the healing salve on both yourself and the other person at all the places where you cut the cords and notice those places heal.

14. If the cord or connection grows back, cut it again and reapply the Gold Light Healing Salve.

    Cords or connections immediately reattaching or regrowing themselves are not unusual. This is a process you are learning, with no right or wrong way to proceed. Relax. Breathe.

15. Continue with step #13 until all the cords are all cut, salve is ap-

plied to each of the wounded areas, healing occurs, and you are feeling peaceful.

16. Thank the other person for their willingness to participate. Release the person and watch that person disappear from the Gold Light Bubble.

17. Allow the Gold Light Bubble to dissolve. Breathe. Relax. Thank yourself. Thank Creator Source. Congratulate yourself!

Notebook: Write your experience in your notebook.

How to deal with a person who refuses to work with you:

At step #7 you may experience the person refusing to come into the Gold Light Bubble to do the work with you. It may help to ask a Guide, Master, or Angel to come into the Bubble with you to lend their support. Often that helps to resolve the "energy" and reduce the wariness of the other person. If that doesn't help, you can ask the other person's Higher Self to come into the Bubble with you and ask for the Higher Self's assistance with the process. Often that helps to resolve the issue.

At step #12 you may experience the person refusing to have the cords cut, wanting to keep those cords intact. It may help to ask a Guide, Master, or Angel to come into the Bubble with you and the other person to lend their support. If that doesn't help, you can ask the other person's Higher Self to come into the Bubble with you and ask for the Higher Self's assistance in the process. Often that helps to resolve the issue.

If none of these recommendations help with the stalemate, let go of the person for the time being. Thank them for showing up and immediately release them with as much love as you can muster. You can attempt this exercise with that person at some later date. Often the passing of time will resolve the irresolution.

**Lauren's Law #13: "The Universe is all about timing.
So is everything in your life."**

One final word

This exercise is meant to be done *for* yourself, *by* yourself, while cutting cords as connected to another person. Please do not attempt to do this exercise on behalf of someone else, because the results may be unpleasant.

***

RITUAL GROUP MEDITATION EXERCISE TRAVELING IN YOUR ETHERIC BODY TO MT. SHASTA – EXERCISE #4

You can make this your regular practice to attend the ritual group mediation traveling in your etheric body to Mt. Shasta. I encourage you to repeat it often as it will help you with experiences and proficiencies that are potent for your growth.

Tape recorder or cellphone: You can use a tape recorder or a cellphone to make a recording of the original exercise to or go to YouTube to listen to the descriptions.

***

At this point you may "take down"—remove—your Lemurian 6-pointed star formation. As you do so, pay attention to discerning an energy shift. Can you feel the difference?

Notebook: Write down experiences, insights and transformations you had in Class #4. Write down your experiences with the Lemurian Star.

***

The Nine Waves of Creation, Dr. Carl Calleman
I and Thou, Martin Buber
Up from Eden, Ken Wilber
Evolutionary Relationships, Patricia Albere

LIVING IN THE NEW LEMURIA:

EXERCISES, PRACTICES, AND TECHNIQUES

Class #11
Congruence

***

LEMURIAN STAR – MERKABA – SACRED GEOMETRY

Set up your Lemurian Star. You will do the next exercises sitting inside your Lemurian Star formations. Feel the energy. If you wish, you may place crystals inside your formation.

***

CONDUITS and EMPATHS

Many world citizens are becoming empathic and conduits.—*The Lemurian Way*, © 1997 – article "Cracking the Cosmic Egg," pg. 130

Due to the effects of unity consciousness, the 9th wave of creation is producing ever more people who are becoming Conduits and Empaths.

ARE YOU AN EMPATH?

Are you an empath? Have you ever been told that you're "too sensitive" or need to toughen up? Do you feel exhausted and anxious after being in crowds or around certain people? Do you have a sensitivity to light, sound, and smells? Or perhaps it takes you longer to wind down after a long day at work? If you answered, "yes" to these questions you may be an empath.

To determine how empathic you are, you can take the following self-assessment test.

20 question self-assessment test

1. Have I been labeled as "overly sensitive," shy, or introverted?

2. Do I frequently get overwhelmed or anxious?

3. Do arguments or yelling make me ill?

4. Do I often feel like I don't fit in?

5. Am I drained by crowds and need alone time to revive myself?

6. Am I over stimulated by noise, odors, or non-stop talkers?

7. Do I have chemical sensitivities or can't tolerate scratchy clothes?

8. Do I prefer taking my own car places so I can leave early if I need to?

9. Do I overeat to cope with stress?

10. Am I afraid of becoming suffocated by intimate relation-ships?

11. Do I startle easily?

12. Do I react strongly to caffeine or medications?

13. Do I have a low pain threshold?

14. Do I tend to socially isolate?

15. Do I absorb other people's stress, emotions, or symptoms?

16. Am I overwhelmed by multitasking and prefer doing one thing at a time?

17. Do I replenish myself in nature?

18. Do I need a long time to recuperate after being with difficult people or energy vampires?

19. Do I feel better in small cities or the country than large cities?

20. Do I prefer one-to-one interactions or small groups rather than large gatherings?

To calculate your results:

- If you answered yes to one to five questions, you're at least partially an empath.

- Responding yes to six to ten questions means you have moderate empathic tendencies.

- Responding yes to eleven to fifteen means you have strong empathic tendencies.

- Answering yes to more than fifteen questions means that you are a full-blown empath.

drjudithorloff.com/quizzes/empath-self-assessment-test/

"Empaths are the medicine the world needs, and they can have a profound impact on humanity with their compassion and understanding. As you learn to identify your special talents, you will find that you not only enrich your life, but you can enrich the lives of others too. The key skill is to learn how to take charge of your sensitivities and learn specific strategies to prevent empathy overload."
—Dr. Judith Orloff

* * *

ARE YOU A CONDUIT? WHAT IS A CONDUIT?

A Conduit can feel, sense, and sometimes hear 144,000 people and their difficulties through one's own body and emotions.

What is the objective of being a Conduit? To help balance some of the planet's difficulties and those of its inhabitants. To "walk a mile in someone else's shoes" which is a definition of compassion.

You can read the article "Are you a Conduit?" on my website.
thymelauren.wixsite.com/thymely-one/single-post/2017/06/28/are-you-a-conduit

If you want to volunteer to become a Conduit, which is a life-long vocation of working for the planet by balancing energy arising from 144,000 others, open your heart and solar plexus and ask. You might want to check in with your Higher Self before you make this weighty decision.

***

DETACHMENT: NOTICING WITHOUT JUDGING EXERCISE #31

Notebook: Set aside a special time each day to write down your observations.

Steps:
- Notice how you feel when alone.

- Notice how you feel when you are around someone else such as a family member, friend, stranger in public, or someone on tv or the internet.

- Notice without judgment. Notice with curiosity and interest.

- Did you feel differently when you were in the presence of someone else?

- What was the difference? Physical, mental, emotional, psychological, spiritual? Did you feel lighter or heavier? Happier or less happy? Was there no change?

- Notice how you feel each day, without judgment.

- Take time to sit with yourself and an emotion. Do your feelings and emotions shift or change throughout the day?

- If you can, take a walk. Notice how you feel when you are in a particular environment. Describe that.

- Notice an object and put a label on it such as attractive or not, utilitarian or not, or any other label you can think of.

- Then remove your label and notice how you feel about the object then. Did the object change? Did you change? Was it easy to remove the label or not?

- Practice with as many objects as you can – natural and man-made.

> *"Just because I feel bad or experience unpleasant things doesn't mean I am bad."*

Notice and write it all down in your notebook.

***

EMOTIONAL CONGRUENCE

As within, so without.
Notice.
Feel the truth in your body.
Do your emotions match your behavior?
Honesty—tell the truth as fast as you can.

Lauren's Law #18: "Tell the truth... as fast as you can with kindness and compassion."

Lauren's Law #19: "There is no such thing as a lie, not even a little white lie."

HEARTMATH

"Recent discoveries ranging from human evolution and genetics to the new science of neuro-cardiology (the bridge between the brain and the heart) have overturned 150 years of thinking when it comes to the way we think of ourselves, our origin, and our capabilities."—Gregg Braden, founding member of *www.Heart-Math.org*

HeartMath's research demonstrates that different patterns of heart activity have different effects on your thoughts and behaviors. Teaching you how to achieve self-regulation is the mission of Inner Balance of HeartMath's technology, with a trainer showing you how to calm yourself, relieving stress and giving you more control over your emotions.

Sign up to learn at *www.HeartMath.org* to learn the process.

BECOME A GLOBAL COHERENCE EMISSARY

You can also join the GCI community and collectively we can make an evolutionary leap working as a group, to a more compassionate, cooperative and peaceful way of being.

Global Coherence Initiative (GCI)   HeartMath Institute
www.heartmath.org/gci/

***

PHYSICAL CONGRUENCE – FENG SHUI

There are ways to ensure being physically congruent. To eat healthfully so your body is satisfied. To exercise so that your body is strong and resilient.

To sleep well so that you are rested. There is another method, Feng Shui, you can use to harmonize and blend with your physical surroundings *and* to make a change in your circumstances.

[When people visit my home, they invariably exclaim about the beauty and peacefulness of my place.]

Feng Shui is an ancient Chinese method of harmonizing the physical space around you and bringing it into alignment with your life. Energy, known as Chi, is enhanced and empowered by your environment. Energy will be created, organized and compartmentalized as you set up your space using Feng Shui.

Feng Shui uses correspondences as did the ancient Egyptians and countless others. You will be working with the energies of plants, objects, and the unseen, while the connections that are made between the energetic objects and your life could be considered amazing, even magical.

For example, the correspondence of the yellow yarn you used to create your Lemurian star changed the energy when sitting inside the Star. The yarn is simply yellow yarn, yet the yarn when made into a six-sided geometric figure transformed the energy corresponding to sacred geometry and Merkabas, thus bringing that energy into your space and your awareness.

ESP, especially clairsentience, is particularly helpful with Feng Shui. As you move objects around, put them up, take them down, or remove them entirely, you will notice shifts both in how you and the room feel. The more you practice, the more you will feel the changes as you move objects around, especially if an object feels "good" or "right" versus unpleasant in that room or space. Although I am going to teach you how to work systematically with your space, Feng Shui can work in ultra-simple ways as well. I discovered that important shifts happen in a space that is clean, organized and tidy. When I lived with my roommate Melanie, I noticed that when Melanie's bedroom and clothes closet got messy, her dating prospects and finances dwindled. When Melanie cleaned those at my urging, her prospects improved immediately.

Magically you can create something you desire simply by washing the floor, cleaning out a closet or garage, or giving away stuff you don't use or need. The phrase "Cleanliness is next to Godliness" comes to mind.

As you renovate your space (home or office) using Feng Shui, elements of your life will flourish in tandem, including fame, wealth and abundance, relationships, health, family, friends, travel, and creativity. You may feel a shift as you take a picture off a wall, hang other pictures up, change a color scheme to one that corresponds to that area, or remove incompatible items. You may also feel a shift as you add items that are correspondences—such as a beautifully framed picture of 2 swans in your marriage area, photos of your children in your family area, or a green bedspread in your health area. As you "Feng Shui" your space, you will intuit the change and then start to notice shifts in that area of your life as well including new relationships, increased financial abundance, improved health, and so on.

FENG SHUI EXERCISE #32

Whenever I use Feng Shui to transform a space corresponding to one's life, I start with a drawing that shows the front door in relation to all the other rooms. If you would like me to Feng Shui your home or office, draw a simple design of your home, using square blocks of space for rooms and indicate what each room is used for. You can also use a fan shape. Include hallways. Indicate where the front and back doors are. The front door is the door you mainly use to enter and exit your home or office. Indicate if there is a staircase.

Send the design to me. I will create a Feng Shui chart and mail it to you with instructions. If you live outside the USA, the easiest way would be to scan your drawing and email the scanned document to me and I will email the results back to you.

Step 1: Draw a design of your space and send it to me. I will then do a free

session for you with suggestions about the elements of each room with recommendations for what you can do to change and improve it.

**Step 2: In the meantime, while you're waiting for your chart, keep your
house, car, garage and office clean and tidy.** Clean up dirt and dust which
stops Chi from flowing easily into your life. Organize cabinets, closets, car,
office and garage. Pick up items and put them away in closets or drawers.

Throw away all dead or dying flowers and plants. Clean flowerpots and vases.
Throw away all artificial flowers and plants; they have no Chi and gather dust.
Remove all plants from bedrooms as they interfere with energy.

Extraneous items will stop the flow of Chi. Give away anything that you are
no longer using.

Step 3: I will send you a chart for your space indicating colors, shapes, materials (metal, wood, etc.), and images to be utilized. You can relocate items
you already have from one area to another, as appropriate, rather than throw
them away and to save money. You can also utilize thrift stores, garage sales,
and *www.freecycle.com / www.trashnothing.com* to get items cheaply or free.
Cost is not critical here. *Correspondences* are vital. After completing your Feng
Shui exercise, feel free to donate leftover items. They may not "fit" anywhere
and can clog up the Chi.

Step 4: Feel free to make changes on your own, using the tips provided for
you. The descriptions included are merely a starting point to work from as
you develop your own space in a way that is deeply personal.

Step 5: Don't overburden your space with too much stuff. Imagine a Zen
Garden. Keep the space elegantly simple. Do you own stuff? Or does stuff
own you? George Carlin has a funny riff about "**Stuff**" on YouTube.
Feng Shui can be complicated, yet simplicity is desirable.

Lauren's Law #3: "If it's easy, it's right."

[One client had an overabundance of stuff and resisted recommendations. The energy of the place felt like clogged plumbing while her romantic life, health and finances suffered—until she wanted to move and sold most of her possessions. Then those areas of her life improved significantly!]

Here are some general ideas:

1. The front and back doors of a house shall not face each other, otherwise the airflow will take away your wealth and affect your family fortune.

2. The bathroom door shall not be opposite to the front door. Since the entrance door is the air inlet of your house, a bathroom door facing it will let in the bad air.

3. The kitchen door shall not face the bedroom door. The bedroom, a place for rest, is supposed to be peaceful and free from water, fire, etc. Water and fire are used every day in the kitchen.

4. The bedroom door shall not face the front door. Since the bedroom is a place for rest, it should be quiet and private. The front door, where your family and friends come in and out, can break the peace of bedroom and affect your health.

5. The kitchen door and the bathroom door shall not be opposite to each other. The kitchen is a place for cooking food while the bathroom is full of stale air. The two facing each other can pollute the kitchen air, and even endanger the health of the hostess.

6. Doors to storage areas shall not face the bedroom door. The storage areas where sundries are piled up have bad air which can lower the air quality of the bedroom.

7. If your home has two doors facing each other, you need to cure it as much as possible. Since the two doors inside are very close to each other, they can have a great impact on the Chi field while the impact on Feng Shui is not to be ignored.

8. Two doors facing each other in your home can easily bring you disputes and disasters, especially if your bedroom door is facing the bathroom. The bathroom/toilet is the place for excretion. Once it faces any door, you may suffer from bad luck and illness. The best way to cure this pattern is to change the location of the bathroom door. If unworkable, hang a curtain on the bedroom door or put some charms in the bedroom, such as a Chinese knot and peony painting. Five-emperor coins, a kind of Feng Shui item which can bring in better luck for wealth and ward off unpleasant energy, are also an effective cure for this pattern. If there are two opposite doors in your home, you can put five-emperor coins under the two doors on the inside or hang two mirrors or a Bagua facing each other on opposite walls. These items can be found inexpensively at Ebay or Amazon.

***

RITUAL GROUP MEDITATION EXERCISE TRAVELING IN YOUR ETHERIC BODY TO MT. SHASTA – EXERCISE #4

This is the time to practice attending the ritual group meditation as you did at the end of Class #1. I encourage you to repeat it often as it will stimulate your growth.

Tape recorder or cellphone: you can use a tape recorder or a cellphone to make a recording of the original exercise to or go to YouTube to listen to the descriptions.

At this point you may "take down"—remove—your Lemurian 6-pointed star formation. As you do so, pay attention to discerning an energy shift. Can you feel the difference?

Notebook: Write down experiences, insights and transformations you had in this class. Write down your experiences with the Lemurian Star.

✳✳✳

[1] *www.findhorn.org*
[2] Lauren's permaculture farm, *Cosmic Grandma Wisdom* © 2017
Science of Self-Empowerment, Gregg Braden

LIVING IN THE NEW LEMURIA:

EXERCISES, PRACTICES, AND TECHNIQUES

Class #12
The Big Picture

Welcome to the twelfth and final class of a series designed to assist you in using The Lemurian Way in your life. This class focuses on The Big Picture and the acceleration of your journey.

***

LEMURIAN STAR – MERKABA – SACRED GEOMETRY

Please seat yourself within the gold star. Feel the energy inside. You may wish to include crystals in your formation.

***

YOUR JOURNEY

These classes have been teaching you to feel and intuit Creator Source and Divine Energy within yourself, to pay attention, and to discern. Along the way you have been introduced to simple yet powerful exercises. This final class marks the end of these classes and a continuation of your life-long journey, one meant to enlighten you, friends, family, clients and students. The classes are tools to help build your unique structure, as you would with a hammer, saw and chisel, only from the inside out.

Chinese proverb: "Give a man a fish and you feed him for a day. Teach a man to fish and you feed him for a lifetime."

Looking at the Big Picture—"Einstein's Quantum Riddle [what he called 'spooky action at a distance' is where everything seems to be connected to everything else]. Join scientists on Nova as they grab light from across the universe to prove quantum entanglement is real."[1] from *PBS.org/Nova/EinsteinsQuantumRiddle*

What else is science discovering to be real?

YOU ARE INVITED TO PARTICIPATE IN A STUDY OF HUMAN CONSCIOUSNESS AS EXPERIENCED THROUGH THE 9th WAVE

Dr. Carl Calleman invites us to explore and deepen our connection to the 9th wave on his website calleman.com. "If we as a species, are going to get back to a state of unity with the cosmos, nature and each other we will need to develop practices that can enhance our resonance with it. It is in fact necessary that we make the quantum shift from focusing on me to focusing on we... To explore this new wave (since 2011) and the effects it has on human consciousness you are invited to participate in this study to further substantiate it and help us get more clarity regarding its nature. This is not limited to shamans, mediums & psychics, teachers, psychologists and therapists within their own field of expertise but is also for anybody with the focus on manifesting the destiny of humanity.

...If you would like to share your experiences with us, we are also interested in your findings by compiling information of relevance to the Ninth Wave. Your descriptions and personal information will be treated as anonymous and will not be forwarded to any other party.

...If you would like to participate in such a study, while tracking the ninth wave in your life, please go here:
www.calleman.com/experiencing-the-9th-wave-influence-in-our-life/

...As members of the Test Group, all the spreadsheets you will need to work with are in the links provided. For maximum efficiency, participants are asked to follow the Ninth Wave through at least three (3) such cycles of 36 days each." — Calleman.com

WHAT IS AN "EVOLUTIONARY" RELATIONSHIP?

"For millennia, spirituality has been a deeply personal pursuit—monks on mountaintops and yogis in caves. But the world is more social than ever, and interconnectedness is transforming everything, from our family lives to work. Today, we need a spirituality that focuses more on *we* than *me*. In her book *Evolutionary Relationships*, Patricia Albere draws on more than four decades of teaching work to introduce a new spirituality called *mutual awakening* that you can explore with a friend, lover, spouse, or partner. With practices to guide you and lessons to inspire you, this book helps you become more available to yourself, your partner, and our world.

...Life is defined by relationships—we're deeply social creatures. But not all relationships are created equal. An 'Evolutionary Relationship' is one that drives us, challenges us, compels us to grow and evolve. It is a consciously created connection that is formed between two or more people who mutually commit to explore and develop higher states of perception and awareness together.

> "…*Evolutionary Relationships* will show you how to find and amplify the 'evolutionary relationships' in your own life. Perhaps more importantly, it will show you how to transform any committed relationship—whether with a spouse, a lover, a partner, a close friend, or family member—into a dynamic engine for mutual evolution."
> —from Patricia Albere's book *Evolutionary Relationships*

DISCOVER MUTUAL AWAKENING

"Are you sensing there are higher possibilities of love, energy and creativity you could activate for yourself and the world…if only you knew how?

…We are living in times of unprecedented political and social upheaval, fear, division and uncertainty. The landscape that we navigate in our daily lives is ever-changing. The walls of some of our time-honored institutions and firmly held beliefs are crumbling.

…Many of us recognize that our culture's established mindset of 'What's in it for me, at all costs and without consideration for our fellow man and Mother Nature' is neither satisfying us as individuals nor serving humanity.

…If the great mystics, sages and spiritual masters are right – what's required for us to move through these challenges is a shift in consciousness. And the best way to change or improve the circumstances of our world is for all of us to first realize deeply who we are… that we are the world.

…You are invited to a new Mutual Awakening course which begins on Saturday, February 13th, 2021. discovermutualawakening.com

…As Buddhist monk and peace activist, Thich Nhat Hanh, puts it, 'We are here to awaken from the illusion of our separateness.'" —Patricia Albere's website discovermutualawakening.com

NATURE, DEVAS AND FAIRIES, PERMACULTURE, AND 30/30

Although we live with nature, observe and attempt to emulate it—we cannot improve on it. We do not steward or guard the earth. If we observe what countless generations have done with the Earth, in trying to improve on nature, we have made things worse on our planet. We can, however, work with Devas (celestial beings similar to angels, not to be confused with Creator Source), that control forces of nature such as fire, air, wind, land, plants, etc. The Findhorn Foundation in Scotland has become world-famous for their work with Devas.[2]

In my article, "My Life with Fairies and Devas", I explores my first-hand experiences:

thymelauren.wixsite.com/thymely-one/single-post/2017/04/17/my-life-with-fairies-and-devas

There are local Devas, such as those who work with a specific plant or animal. Then there are all-encompassing Devas who work with a large area up to hundreds of miles in diameter. If you wish to work with Devas, all you need to do is ask aloud, to call one in with respect. In my experience, they are eager to be of service. Their jobs are to help the planet and they want you to call on them. If you are psychically attuned you may find it easier to see, hear or feel a Deva. Once you have called one in, you will find it easier to work with Devas from then on.

To work with nature, you can also plant food gardens using Permaculture, an ancient form of growing food becoming popular worldwide, while caring for the local soil, trees and beneficial insects and animals. I organically gardened for 30 years, then owned and operated a permaculture farm on Whidbey Island in the state of Washington for 7 years.[3]

Fungi including mycelium are one of the primary building blocks on our planet with a main fungi Deva in charge. A movie worth watching is Fabulous Fungi. [4]

30/30 is an organization designed to conserve at least 30% of U.S. land and ocean by 2030, a part of an international push for conservation aiming to protect biodiversity and mitigate climate change impacts.[5]

HEALTH - ONE SIZE DOES NOT FIT ALL

We each live in our own separate universe. What works for someone else may not work for you and vice versa. What you and your body need, requires trial and error, discernment and paying attention to resonance on your part.

Lauren's Law #24: "Pay attention as if your life depends on it. It does."

In my book *Alternatives for Everyone*, I detail many alternative, non-traditional, and holistic health care solutions.

RECOMMENDATIONS

If you eat meat and poultry, eat only grass fed.

Avoid eating all grains, dairy, sugar, eggs, and soy. Read all product labels to see if the item contains these ingredients.

Functional medicine doctors advise us to avoid eating all grains which cause many health issues.

"The Functional Medicine model is an individualized, patient-centered, science-based approach that empowers patients and practitioners to work together to address the underlying causes of disease and promote optimal wellness. It requires a detailed understanding of each patient's genetic, biochemical, and lifestyle factors and leverages that data to direct personalized treatment plans that lead to improved patient outcomes. By addressing the root cause(s), rather than symptoms, practitioners become oriented to identifying the complexity of disease. They may find one condition has many different causes and, likewise, one cause may result in many different conditions. As a result, Functional Medicine treatment targets the specific manifestations of disease in each individual."

—Institute of Functional Medicine

"Grains by default are designed to chemically protect themselves from predation. We are the predators. They don't want to be eaten by us. They [certainly] don't want to be eaten into extinction. They have what we call a class of proteins. Gluten is one of those proteins. Lectins are another class of proteins. There are a number of different classes of proteins that I categorized as century proteins. These are proteins that the seed itself has a purpose, to shut down the digestion of animal predators. It's to create inflammation in animal predators as a deterrent from [being eaten]."

—Dr. Peter Osborne from his book *No Grain, No Pain*

"In Grain Brain, renowned neurologist David Perlmutter, MD, exposes a finding that's been buried in the medical literature for far too long: carbs are destroying your brain. Even so-called healthy carbs like whole grains can cause dementia, ADHD, epilepsy, anxiety, chronic headaches, depression, decreased libido, and much more."

—*Grain Brain*

Anthony William, in his world-famous book *Medical Medium*, tells us that eggs have been used for a hundred years or more to create vaccines, so eggs are suspect, plus most people have egg sensitivities. If you must eat them, eat only grass-raised chicken and duck eggs. "The biggest issues with eggs is they're a prime food for cancer and other cysts, fibroids, tumors and nodules. Women with polycystic ovary syndrome (PCOS), breast cancer, or other cysts and tumors should avoid eating eggs altogether. Eggs also cause inflammation and allergies, feed viruses, bacteria, yeast, mold, Candida and other fungus, and trigger edema in the lymphatic system."
—Anthony William, *Medical Medium*, p. 281.

Take health supplements daily. Because of the coronavirus outbreak, strengthening our immune systems is vital to our health while supplements can enhance autoimmunity. Some supplements contain fillers and other ingredients that must be avoided to maintain health. You can research what to watch out for in Dr. Tom O'Bryan's book *The Autoimmune Fix*

When you can, grow your own food — organically. If that is not possible, you can grow sprouts and herbs in your kitchen, living room or patio. Anything fresh is enormously powerful for your body. Eat as many fresh herbs as possible in salads.

Buy good seed for your garden. Most seed companies have been taken over by chemical companies who change the DNA of seed, patent them, and keep them from common usage. Some ethical seed companies which sell organic and heirloom seeds are Territorial Seed Company, Johnny's Seed, and Gardens Alive.

Drink spring water (if you can find some where the ground water isn't polluted) or water purified by reverse osmosis. Keep water stored in glass or stainless steel, not plastic, as it presents many problems. Wal-Mart has been offering water in plastic bottles that was toxic and also selling water from California which is suffering a drought.

Water pollution is rampant due to these substances: Chlorine (affects the thyroid), Fluoride, (a neurotoxin and an endocrine disruptor), Herbicides, Nitrates, Lead, Mercury (often discharged from refineries, factories, ore extractions, landfill and cropland runoff from fertilizer), Methyl Tertiary Butyl Ether (used in gasoline to reduce carbon monoxide and ozone levels from auto emissions), Perchlorate (a widespread toxic chemical, used in rocket fuel, explosives, and road flares) and Pharmaceuticals. The EPA estimates that the nation's aging and inefficient sewage treatment systems release over 850 billion gallons of untreated wastewater every year.

Where do human waste, household chemicals, pharmaceuticals, personal hygiene products, used water from our sinks, showers, and toilets, and everything else that goes down the drains end up after leaving homes and businesses? In sewers. And what happens when the rain washes pesticides, fertilizers, automotive chemicals, debris, road salts, oil, grease, and chemicals down gutters into those same sewers? The sewage backs up in people's basements, flows onto the streets, in parks, and rivers, lakes, streams, and so on. According to the United Nations, over 80 percent of the world's wastewater flows back into the environment without being treated or reused. That figure reaches as much as 95 percent in some least-developed countries.

Use biodegradable, non-toxic cleaning supplies or make your own.

Use only non-toxic hair and skin care products and cosmetics. Whatever you apply externally is absorbed into the body.

Stop using plastic and use glass containers, bio-bags and cloth shopping bags instead. Plastic injures and poisons wildlife, escapes from landfills into water supplies, consumes priceless energy, leaches into food and drinks, crosses the placenta, and causes reproductive harm and infertility.

Recycle everything. Give away and buy recycled items to and from thrift stores and garage sales and use *www.trashnothing.com* or *www.freecycle.com.*

Avoid getting knee, hip replacement or rotator-cuff surgery. You can instead practice simple exercises found in The Egoscue Method of Health through Motion. [I healed both my knees and avoided painful, costly surgery by doing Egoscue-recommended specific exercises.]

Relax, eat, move, and sleep mindfully from Dr. Rangan Chatterjee's book *How to Make Disease Disappear: The 4 Pillar Plan.*

Protect yourself from dangerous EMF's emitted from your cell phone and laptop with SafeSleeve.

Sign up to use renewable electricity using only solar or wind at Arcadia. The cost to add this feature is minimal [I pay an extra $5.00 month] and they work with your electric company, so you get just one bill. *https://arcadia.com/referral/?promo=lauren7019*

LIVING OUTSIDE THE BOX - THERE IS NO *AWAY*

In our modern world, we desperately need to live "outside the box" to restore health to ourselves and the planet. How can we do it?

"I want to throw this away," yet there is no such thing as AWAY. Garbage dumps are filled to overflowing, containing food scraps, dead plants, and cut flowers that could be composted instead. When put into a municipal dump, these things rot and cause methane which leads to global warming. If you can, find a farm that will take your compost to make into soil. If not, there are bins and composting systems you can buy online to create your own compost for a healthy garden.

"The technical term for…high-tech garbage is e-waste…like TVs and com-

puters (including keyboards, monitors, mouses, printers, scanners and other accessories)…cell phones, DVD players, video cameras and answering machines…any products that use electricity, like refrigerators, toasters, lamps, toys, power drills, and pacemakers… Your typical piece of electronic equipment—especially one like a PC with many circuit boards—may contain up to 8 pounds of lead, along with low levels of mercury, arsenic, cadmium, beryllium and other toxic chemicals."
—from the website How Stuff Works *computer.howstuffworks.com/discarded-old-computer.htm*

Computers, cell phones and other electronics are hazardous to our health. "Cell phone dangers to children: due to developing organs, lower bone density of the skull, lower body weight, and a less effective blood brain barrier, children are especially vulnerable to cell phone radiation. This is even more true for unborn children… Sadly, the Earth, too, suffers from the toxins in cell phones. Mining tin, tantalum, tungsten, and gold for cell phone production causes groundwater contamination as well as human exploitation and brutality in the Democratic Republic of the Congo. Moreover, once a cell phone is discarded, it is shipped to [poverty-stricken] places in the world… like China, India, Pakistan, Vietnam, and the Philippines, where underpaid workers handle the materials and are exposed to the toxins we go to such lengths to avoid ourselves."
—from the website Natural Society, *naturalsociety.com/cell-phone-dangers-safety-cancer-mercury-hazards/*

All cars pollute and create problems in one form or other, including hybrid and electric cars. "Everybody's heard of the controversy over lithium supplies, which are a key component of the lithium-ion battery packs going into EVs [electric vehicles]. Lithium deposits are concentrated in just a few mostly non-western countries (China, Bolivia, Chile). Most experts think there's enough lithium for the foreseeable future, though some of it is in countries hostile to the U.S. (including, as we've recently discovered, Afghanistan). But there is growing concern over another key raw material for the electric car — rare earth minerals. There's a reason they call these minerals "rare"—they

are! But they're also necessary. Neodymium is a vital component of EV motor magnets. According to Reuters, two other minerals—terbium and dysprosium are added to neodymium to allow it to remain magnetic at high temperatures."
– CBS News
cbsnews.com/news/forget-lithium-its-rare-earth-minerals-that-are-in-short-supply-for-evs/

Six problems with electric cars that no one is talking about:
www.autoevolution.com/news/six-problems-with-electric-cars-that-nobody-talks-about-112221.html#:~:text=The%20problem%20with%20electric%20ve-hicles%20is%20that%20lithium,neodymium%20and%20praseodymium%2C%20and%20"a%20touch%20of"%20dysprosium

AH TAY MALKUTH - THE KABBALISTIC CROSS/TREE OF LIFE

Most of the exercises in this course can deal with any problem you may face. Occasionally an adverse energy appears in our lives, showing up as a curse, an abusive person or situation, which cannot be easily expunged by any other method. The *Ah Tay Malkuth* chant is designed to forever banish and remove that influence from your life or that of your client.

The Ah Tay Malkuth has its origin in the Kabbalah, also known as the Tree of Life or Kabbalistic Cross. "The earliest roots of Kabbalah, early Jewish mysticism, are traced to Merkaba mysticism. The Kabbalah began to flourish in Palestine in the 1st century CE and had as its main concern ecstatic and mystical contemplation of the divine throne, or "chariot" (Merkaba), seen in a vision by Ezekiel, the prophet." from Britannica
www.britannica.com/topic/Kabbala

[The entire text of the chant is included at the end of this class after the footnotes. I recommend you save the chant for when you absolutely need it. I have used it only a handful of times in my long career.]

How will you know you are making progress?

Disharmonious feelings happen less often, feel less intense and remain a shorter time.

Harmonious and positive feelings happen oftener, feel deeper, and stay longer.

***

"Before enlightenment, chop wood. Carry water.
After enlightenment, chop wood. Carry water."
– Zen Koan

***

HEALING MEDITATION AT MT. SHASTA CO-CREATION with the 9TH WAVE with unified connection with the Divine –

EXERCISE #33

The 9th and final wave of the Mayan calendar started in 2011. We are now in a period of regeneration and transformation which includes unity, harmony, connection to the Divine Creator Source and conscious co-creation with the Divine according to the Divine Plan.

You are going to do a new exercise instead of the ritual group meditation traveling in your etheric body to Mt. Shasta. Instead, you are going to perform a healing meditation restoring vitality to our stressed planet. This is a potent exercise, one I encourage you to practice often.

Steps:

Remove your logical mind and set it aside. You won't need it for this journey.

> Focus on the images of Mt. Shasta you see on your screen. Say to yourself, "I'm going to Mt. Shasta and I will meet Lemurian friends there." Imagine that your spiritual body is journeying to Mt. Shasta.

> As you arrive, you notice other people including me. When you arrive, you see former and current friends as well as friends who are no longer alive. You reunite with family 7 or more generations back on both sides. A dance ensues while people play music of all kinds as you dance, sing and party.

> You see and then merge with other Lemurians as well as Devas of the earth, animals, plants, amphibians, mycelium, fungi, water, and air.

> You and the others decide spontaneously to clean up fire damage at Mt. Shasta. You spread fresh soil and healthy compost, inoculate soil with mycelium, plant wildflower seeds, and tree saplings. Your celebration becomes a renovation party. As you restore the sacred mountain landscape, you watch the seeds and saplings spring into new life and grow quickly.

> You are in your etheric body which can take you anywhere you wish to go, while you can accomplish actions, deeds and activities at the speed of thought. Creation begins as thought on the etheric plane. You brim with excitement as you realize your capabilities and potential, working on the etheric plane.

> Then you realize that while in your etheric body, you can operate on Earth's etheric plane as well, not limited to the 3-dimensional physical plane.

Restoration can then be accomplished all over the entire Earth with ease as you remember **Lauren's Law #5: "M = ET²"**

First you travel to Paradise, California, where you clean up fire damage, remove burned trees, buildings and cars. You spread fresh soil and healthy compost, inoculating the soil with mycelium, then planting wildflower seeds, tree saplings, even full-grown trees. You watch them grow quickly. You become joyfully aware that you are in the 9th wave of creation which includes conscious co-creation with the Divine. In the energy of the 9th wave on the higher vibration of the etheric plane an eternity can transpire in an instant of 3D earth time.

Then you proceed everywhere on the planet, transforming burned trees in the Amazon forest, dissolving rusted and dilapidated buildings and cars, spreading fresh soil and healthy compost, inoculating soil with mycelium and other fungi, planting wildflower seeds, tree saplings, and full-grown trees.

You visit the seas where you balance acidity in the oceans and restore coral to health. You easily transform the accumulated plastic waste into nourishment for the ocean, allowing it to restore its function of breathing for the planet while saving countless seabirds, kelp, plankton, and aquatic life.

You replace endangered, diminished or extinct species along with Joshua trees, Giant Redwoods and Sequoias, returning them to their proper homes while restoring their habitats. You visit the Amazon where you heal and restore damaged ecosystems, encouraging the jungle to revitalize and expand. You feel the Earth exhale, joyous that it is coming alive once again, then it inhales, knowing it can support all the teeming life on our planet from the microscopic to the largest life forms.

You clean water, air and soil of pollution and restore them to health.

You reduce deserts and restore greenery.

As you restore the planet, you wonder to yourself, "Is this how earth was originally created? By thought and desire?"

You continue to visit all the damaged places on earth, restoring them to health and beauty. The oceans become calmer. The climate of the earth begins to cool. The Arctic, Greenland, and Antarctica return to their normal temperatures.

Finally, you become conscious that energy is abundant and free on the planet, without the need for petroleum products or even green energy. You reach out to connect with scientific, investigative minds to encourage them to achieve free energy for the planet.[6] You smile to yourself at your co-creations, pleased that Earth is returning to its natural health, just as you are doing with yourself.

You realize it is time to leave, to return to your physical body in your separate home. I invite you to come back often now that you know how to find your way. You are connected to Lemurians and all spiritual people as they are connected to you. You are part of a growing community of people unified in love, peace, happiness and conscious co-creation. With every passing day, this unconditional love and unification grows in strength and numbers. On this planet we are all connected as one heart. *Together we are able to heal our planet.*

In a flash you are back in your physical body in your physical home. With a deep breath and a lingering sigh, you thank yourself for your experience. You thank others who attended. You smile remembering your experiences. Now open your eyes and put your logical mind back in place. Feel your feet on the floor and your body seated in your chair. Stretch and come back to present time.

[This exercise was downloaded to me on 11/28/2020 while a class member was reading the Mt. Shasta meditation script to us.]

I hope you found these classes valuable, interesting, and fun! Stay tuned to these exercises coming out on YouTube.

***

[1] Einstein's Quantum Riddle, *www.pbs.org/wgbh/nova/video/einsteins-quantum-riddle/*
[2] *www.findhorn.org*
[3] *www.permaculturenews.org/what-is-permaculture/* Permaculture Foundation
[4] movie "Fabulous Fungi"
[5] 30 x 30 project eos.org/articles/30-by-30-a-push-to-protect-u-s-land-and-water
[6] free energy, Dr. Steven Greer siriusdisclosure.com

Helpful Information

The Nine Waves of Creation, Dr. Carl J. Calleman
Evolutionary Relationships, Patricia Albere
The Egoscue Method of Health through Motion, Pete Egoscue
How To Make Disease Disappear: The 4 Pillar Plan, Dr. Rangan Chatterjee
Cosmic Grandma Wisdom, © 2017 Lauren O. Thyme fairies and devas; permaculture farm
Alternatives for Everyone, © 1988, 2nd edition © 2017 Lauren O. Thyme
Gaia's Garden, Toby Hemenway © 2009
Life Changing Foods, Anthony William (also on YouTube)
Liver Rescue, Anthony William
Cleanse to Heal, Anthony William
Medical Medium, Anthony William
Thyroid Healing, Anthony William

Environmental Working Group *www.ewg.org*
Institute of Functional Medicine *www.ifm.org*
Safe Sleeve *www.SafeSleeve.com*
Arcadia *www.Arcadia.com*

Books based on Functional Medicine practices

The Autoimmune Fix, Dr. Tom O'Bryan (also on YouTube)
You Can Fix Your Brain, Dr. Tom O'Bryan (also on YouTube)
No Grain, No Pain Dr. Peter Osborne (also on YouTube)
Grain Brain, Dr. David Perlmutter, neurologist (also on YouTube)
Blood Sugar Solution, Dr. Mark Hyman. American physician and New York Times best-selling author, founder and medical director of The UltraWellness Center, (also on YouTube)
Put Your Heart In Your Mouth, Natural treatment for Angina, Heart attack, High blood pressure, Stroke, Arrythmia, Peripheral Vascular Disease, Atheroschlerosis
Dr. Natasha Campbell-McBride, MD, MMedisci (neurology), MMedSci (nutrition)
Gut And Psychology Syndrome, Natural Treatment for Autism, Dyspraxia, A.D.D., A.D.H.D., Dyslexia, Depression, Schizophrenia
Dr. Natasha Campbell-McBride, MD
Vegetarianism Explained: Making an Informed Decision, Dr. Natasha Campbell-McBride, MD
Gut and Physiology Syndrome: Natural Treatment for Allergies, Autoimmune Illness, Arthritis, Gut Problems, Fatigue, Hormonal Problems, Neurological Disease and More
    Dr. Natasha Campbell-McBride, MD
The Whole Body Approach To Osteoporosis, Dr. R. Keith McCormick (also on YouTube)

***

AH TAY MALKUTH - THE KABBALISTIC CROSS EXERCISE #34

If you wish, you can burn incense and/or white candles.
Speak loudly and emphatically.

(All persons face east with their palms facing forward)

Ah tay (This Hebrew word means *Thou art...* and acknowledges
Creator Source)
Malkuth (*The Kingdom*)
Ve-Geburah (*and The Power*)
Ve-Gedulah (*and The Glory*)
Lay-Olam (*forever* or *unto all the ages*)
Amen.

In the Name of Names Above All Names
I banish from the space around me
All seeds of evil and cast them out of my aura
Where they shall not trouble this seeker of truth now and for-
ever.

(All persons face south with their palms facing forward)

Ah tay Malkuth
Ve-Geburah
Ve-Gedulah
Lay-Olam
Amen.

In the Name of Names Above All Names
I banish from the space above me
All seeds of evil and cast them out of my aura
Where they shall not trouble this seeker of truth now and for-
ever.

(All persons face west with their palms facing forward)

Ah tay Malkuth
Ve-Geburah
Ve-Gedulah
Lay-Olam
Amen.
In the Name of Names Above All Names
I banish from the space below me
All seeds of evil and cast them out of my aura
Where they shall not trouble this seeker of truth now and for-
ever.

(All persons face north with their palms facing forward)

Ah tay Malkuth
Ve-Geburah
Ve-Gedulah
Lay-Olam
Amen.

In the Name of Names Above All Names
I banish from the space within me
All seeds of evil and cast them out of my aura
Where they shall not trouble this seeker of truth now and for-
ever.

(quite loudly)
Where they shall not trouble this seeker of truth now and forever! **(CLAP HANDS LOUDLY)**

Dragon dreaming:

*dragondreaming.wordpress.com/2015/09/26/draconic-qabalistic-cross-
ritual/#:~:text="The%20ritual%20of%20the%20Qabalistic%20Cross%20is%2
0a,toward%20the%20ideal%20of%20one%20balanced%20"Higher%20Self".*

COMPLETION

Now it's time to return to your physical body in your physical home. Put your logical mind back in place. It's graduation time. Celebrate!!

Thank you for joining me in *Living in the New Lemuria*.

Feel free to contact me for any reason or to say Hi at *thyme.lauren@gmail.com*

I wish you Gold Light Blessings on your continuing journey, riding the 9th wave as an Enlightened Surfer on our beloved planet.

Hugs

Lauren O. Thyme